LOKMATA
AHILYABAI

LOKMATA
AHILYABAI

Arvind Javlekar

Ocean Books Pvt. Ltd.

ISO 9001:2015 Publishers

Published by
Ocean Books (P) Ltd.
4/19 Asaf Ali Road,
New Delhi-110 002 (INDIA)
e-mail: prabhatbooks@gmail.com

ISBN 81-88322-08-3
LOKMATA AHILYABAI
by Shri Arvind Javlekar

Edition
2025

Price
₹ 300.00 (Rupees Three Hundred only)

Printed at
Narula Printers, Delhi

श्रीमती सुमित्रा महाजन
Smt. SUMITRA MAHAJAN

राज्य मंत्री
मानव संसाधन विकास मंत्रालय
(महिला एवं बाल विकास
विभाग)
भारत सरकार
नई दिल्ली–110 001
MINISTER OF STATE FOR
HUMAN RESOURCE
DEVELOPMENT
(DEPT. OF WOMEN &
CHILD DEVELOPMENT)
GOVERNMENT OF INDIA
NEW DELHI-110 001

प्रस्तावना

पिछले वर्ष महिला सशक्तिकरण वर्ष के अवसर पर जब महिलाओं के लिए प्रेरणादायी आधुनिक भारत की प्रमुख स्त्रियों, लोकमाता देवी अहिल्याबाई होल्कर, छत्रपति शिवाजी की माता जीजाबाई, झाँसी की रानी लक्ष्मीबाई, अपने न्यायिक अधिकारों के लिए लड़नेवाली तमिलनाडु की देवी कण्णगी तथा स्वतंत्रता संग्राम नागालैंड की रानी गाइडिन्ल्यू के नाम पर पाँच राष्ट्रीय स्त्री शक्ति पुरस्कारों की स्थापना की गई थी। तभी यह विचार भी मन में उत्पन्न हुआ था कि पुरस्कार के साथ ही मातृशक्ति द्वारा किए गए अद्‍भुत कार्यों से भी नई पीढ़ी को परिचित कराया जाना चाहिए। विपरीत परिस्थितियों में भी धैर्य के साथ मार्गक्रमण करते हुए सफलता के शिखर पर पहुँचनेवाली इन स्त्रियों का जीवन–चरित्र जब नई पीढ़ी के समक्ष रखा जाएगा तो स्वाभाविक रूप से उन्हें भी विपरीत परिस्थितियों से संघर्ष करने की प्रेरणा मिलेगी। इसी विचार से इन महान् विभूतियों के जीवन–चरित्र को सरल तथा सुबोध भाषा में लोगों तक पहुँचाने का विचार उत्पन्न हुआ।

इसी परिप्रेक्ष्य में इस वर्ष लोकमाता देवी अहिल्या के जीवन तथा कार्यों को अभिव्यक्त करनेवाली पुस्तक 'लोकमाता अहिल्याबाई' प्रकाशित हो रही है।

पुस्तक के लेखक श्री अरविंद जवलेकर ने सरल भाषा में देवी अहिल्या के जीवन पर विविध पहलुओं को पाठकों के सम्मुख रखने का प्रयास किया है।

यह पुस्तक नई पीढ़ी के पाठकों के लिए उपयोगी तथा प्रेरणादायक सिद्ध होगी, ऐसी अपेक्षा है।

८ मार्च, २००२

(सुमित्रा महाजन)

Contents

1
Holkar Kingdom in Malwa Province

Western region of India's heartland Madhya Pradesh is known as Malwa province. It has common borders with Rajasthan, Gujarat and Maharashtra and is nurtured by the sacred rivers like Narmada, Kshipra and Shivana. Because of its fertile land and moderate climate, this province has always been rich and prosperous. It is said about Malwa that it has no paucity of bread and water. Moreover, people of this region believe that Malwa has always remained safe from natural disasters because virtuous king like emperor Vikramaditya, promoter of art and culture king like Bhoj and pious and saintly rulers like Lokmata Ahilyabai Holkar have ruled this province.

The same richness and prosperity, however, had made Malwa a target of foreign invasions as well. During the regime of emperor Chandragupt Vikramaditya, Sakas and Huns invaded Malwa many times, but they were no match against the might of Chandragupt Vikramaditya. But the circumstances changed with time and Malwa became a part of mighty Mughal empire during medieval period.

As the Mughal empire declined in strength towards the later part of Seventeenth century, Mughal Subedars (local rulers appointed by the Mughal emperors to run individual state) became unruly and despotic. Those days, Malwa too had a Subedar named Daya Bahadur, appointed by the Mughal emperor Mohammed Shah. Contrary to his name Daya (kindness), the Subedar was very cruel. Subjects of Malwa were crying for a saviour under his atrocities.

For the collection of land revenue in the region north to the river Narmada, Mughals had appointed an official named Rao Nandlal. He was very brave and religious person. With an army under him, Nandlal stayed in Indore.

Rao Nandlal was very sad to see the plight of the people under the reign of Daya Bahadur. He tried hard to convince Daya Bahadur to leave the path of cruelty and take to the right course, but he could not succeed. Rao Nandlal even approached the Mughal emperor and informed him about the atrocities of Daya Bahadur, but the emperor Mohammed Shah was too powerless to deal with the Subedar. Consequently, Rao Nandlal was forced to return empty- handed from Delhi.

All these exercises of Rao Nandlal made Daya Bahadur indignant. But at the same time, inability of the emperor to do anything against him made Daya Bahadur even more daring. Though Daya Bahadur was angry with Rao Nandlal, but for his strength and friendly terms with other chieftains of the region, he could not harm Rao Nandlal.

As a later course of action, Rao Nandlal stopped collecting revenue from the public that he used to do and send to the Mughal emperor. Instead of sending revenue, Rao Nandlal wrote, "Because of your inability to curb Subedar Daya Bahadur, he is inflicting all kinds of atrocities on your subjects. So, it is no longer possible for me to recover taxes from the public and send to you." Rao Nandlal had thought that his action perhaps might compel the emperor to take some action against Daya Bahadur. But even this effort of Rao Nandlal proved futile.

Whilst Rao Nandlal was worried about the welfare of the people in Malwa, Peshwa Bajirao had been carrying out expeditions for the expansion of his Hindu empire. Dejected by the passivity and inability of the Mughal emperor, Rao Nandlal saw a ray of hope in Bajirao Peshwa.

In a letter, Rao Nandlal made Bajirao Peshwa aware about the situation prevailing in Malwa, plight of its people and requested him to get the people rid of the atrocities of the Mughal empire and establish *Hindavi* self-rule in the province. Rao Nandlal also assured Bajirao Peshwa of his full co-operation in case Maratha army invaded Malwa. Bajirao Peshwa had been waiting for the appropriate opportunity since long. As soon as he received the message of Rao Nandlal, Bajirao Peshwa sent a twelve thousand strong army led by Malhar Rao Holkar to launch an attack on Malwa. Keeping his promise, Rao Nandlal extended his full co-operation to Maratha army in order to gain an entry in Malwa.

Mughal Subedar Daya Bahadur was badly confounded when he heard about the invasion of Malwa by Maratha army. Even his pride felt shattered. He immediately rushed to Rao Nandlal and requested him not to co-operate the Marathas against the Mughals. He tried every trick, but he could not shake the determination of Rao Nandlal. In very clear words, Rao Nandlal told him that he would no longer co-operate with the Mughal empire.

Thus, out of compulsion, Mughal Subedar came with a huge Mughal army to confront Malhar Rao Holkar. Daya Bahadur took position along with his twenty-five thousand strong army in Mandav Ghat. He laid many mines throughout the Ghat area, which caused severe loss to the Maratha army. Rao Nandlal then suggested the Maratha army to launch a fresh attack via Bhairo Ghat. At last, a fierce battle took place between the Mughal and Maratha armies on October 12, 1731

in Tirala near Dhar. Mughal Subedar Daya Bahadur was killed in the battle, while the remaining Mughal army ran away. Thus, Malhar Rao Holkar took over the control of Malwa province.

Bajirao Peshwa appointed Malhar Rao Holkar as the Subedar of Malwa province. Conferring full honour on Rao Nandlal, Malhar Rao granted him all the rights that he had enjoyed during Mughal rule. Thus, Malhar Rao Holkar took control of the whole Malwa province and established *Hindavi* self-rule there. As Malhar Rao constantly had to accompany Bajirao Peshwa on military expeditions. He appointed his loyal subordinate Gangadhar Yashwant Chandrachur as the Diwan of Malwa and gave him all the administrative powers of the province. He himself began to assist Bajirao Peshwa in his military expeditions to expand the boundaries of the Maratha empire.

2

Daughter of Maharashtra, Daughter-in-law of Malwa

In the beginning of the Eighteenth century, there was a small hamlet named Chauri in the Beed Tehsil near Aurangabad city of Maharashtra. Manakoji Shinde was the *Patil* (chief) of that hamlet. Though Manakoji was not prosperous economically, yet he was rich in virtues like good moral character, piety and cultured behaviour. Like Manakoji, his wife Sushilabai was also very pious in nature and cared for her family affectionately.

In that cultured family of Manakoji Shinde, a radiant girl child was born birth on May 31, 1725. She was named Ahilya by her parents. Since her childhood, Ahilya showed superb intelligence. Manakoji made proper arrangement of Ahilya's education.

Great achievers have a solid foundation right in their childhood. Consecration of the mind that takes place during childhood is the lifetime treasure of a human being. Consecrations and the culture that Ahilyabai's parents infused in her mind became the basis of her public life later on.

Parents of Ahilyabai not only taught her how to read and

write, but also trained her as per the prevailing convention and through the medium of *Pauranic* and folktales, in religious, moral and practical knowledge. Apart from the intellectual training, Ahilyabai received physical and military training also. She had already been trained in horse riding, archery and fencing right from her childhood.

All that hard training and education had inculcated in Ahilyabai's personality a strong sense of self-confidence. Knowledge and confidence gave her face an extraordinary glow. Just at a raw age of eight, her brilliant personality had begun to dazzle the eyes of the people.

Everyday, Ahilyabai used to go with her mother to the Shiv temple of the village to worship and to listen to the *Pauranic* tales. One day in the morning, while Ahilyabai and her mother were entering the temple, they happened to meet two royal men at the gate. Those royal men were none other than Bajirao Peshwa and his commander Malhar Rao Holkar. *En route* their military expedition, they had camped near village Chauri along with their forces. Both the commanders had been taking a morning walk and had strolled towards Shiv temple holding discussion about the expedition. While they were returning after having *Darshan* of Lord Shiva, their attention was caught by that spinster girl, who was entering the temple carrying worship saucer in her hands. Sighting of an extremely brilliant young girl during an early hour of dawn at the onset of the expedition, appeared to the commanders as an auspicious omen. Moreover, the radiant beauty of the girl left both of them spellbound. They held a small chat with Ahilyabai and received her introduction and returned to their camps impressed by her personality.

Subedar Malhar Rao found it hard to part with the impressive personality of Ahilyabai. In the unearthly personality of Ahilyabai, Malhar Rao saw a bright future of

his kingdom. Again and again, a thought kept spurting his mind that all of his worries might end only if that girl could become his daughter-in-law.

His thought was natural, because for past many days he had been worrying constantly about the future of his kingdom. From his queen consort Gautamabai, Malhar Rao had a son, Khande Rao, who was the natural successor of his kingdom after him. But Khande Rao was totally lacking in the virtues that a king should possess. Despite hard efforts, Khande Rao could neither finish his education nor learn the martial art. He had been a matter of worry for his father due to his stubborn and contumelious nature. Hence, to see a brilliant girl like Ahilyabai, it was natural for him to think that such a cultured girl could transform his son and impart some virtues in him that a good ruler should have; if she would accept to become his daughter-in-law.

As soon as the two commanders reached their camps, Malhar Rao intimated Bajirao about his thought and sought his opinion. Bajirao too was greatly impressed by Ahilyabai, so he liked the idea very much. At once, they sent some messengers to summon Ahilyabai's father Manakoji Shinde. Intimating Manakoji about the desire of Malhar Rao, Bajirao sought the hands of his daughter for Malhar Rao's son Khande Rao. This unprecedented proposal left Manakoji speechless. Since long, he had also been seeking a suitable groom for his daughter; but he had not the slightest idea that proposal from such a high-ranking person might come for the daughter of a common man like him. So, it was natural for him to be left speechless. After a little thought, he said, "It is indeed a great fortune for us that a superior man like you has sought my daughter for his son. But we are ordinary people; it is beyond our capacity to marry our daughter to your son with pomp and show that suit your status." Malhar Rao said in consoling voice,

"Do not worry Manakoji. Your daughter is so brilliant and meritorious, that all the wealth and kingdom are nothing before her. You need not worry at all about the expenses of the marriage. We do not expect or demand any dowry. Only give us your daughter Ahilya, we see in her the future of our kingdom." Now Manakoji had nothing more to say, he gladly accepted the proposal.

Thus, in the year 1733, marriage of Malhar Rao Holkar's son Khande Rao with Ahilyabai took place amidst great fanfare. Bajirao Peshwa was himself present alongwith his wife on the occasion to bless the newly married couple. Malhar Rao was feeling fortunate to get such a virtuous daughter-in-law. He presented her with ornaments of gold weighing two hundred *Tolas*. Thus, that brilliant girl of a little hamlet Chauri came to Malwa as the daughter-in-law of the Subedar of the province.

3

Separation from Husband

After marriage, when a young girl steps into the house of her in-laws, she cherishes many dreams about her future. Ahilyabai was born in an ordinary family. She could not have imagined that one day she would become the daughter-in-law of Subedar Malhar Rao Holkar. Naturally, she too might have been cherishing many dreams about her future. But when she came to know about her husband Khande Rao closely, she was greatly frustrated.

Undoubtedly, Ahilyabai's husband was not exactly upto her expectations. Khande Rao was neither interested in governing the kingdom, nor in military expeditions. He also stayed away from education and weapons. Playing uselessly and vagrancy were his favourite pastime. If Ahilyabai were an ordinary woman, she would have given away to the circumstances. But Ahilyabai was not an ordinary woman. She was greatly capable of finding a way out of extremely adverse situations. Hence, instead of mourning over her shattered dream, she stood firm to face the circumstances and took a resolution to transform her husband.

Ahilyabai might have not received expected love from her husband, but her mother-in-law Gautamabai and father-

in-law showered her with parental love and affection. Ahilyabai too regarded them as her real parents and served them with love. Everyday, she would get up before the dawn and after her routine tasks, prayers etc., she used to spend her day in the domestic chores and service of her in-laws. At night also, she used to tell *Pauranic* moral tales to her husband before retiring and tried to develop culture in him.

In the married life of a man, wife plays the same role as is played by his parents in his childhood to consecrate his life. If the wife is able, she can show her husband the righteous path, consecrating his life. Conversely, if the wife is stupid, she turns her own as well as her family's life to hell.

Ahilyabai was an able wife. Besides knowledge, humanity and a serving attitude, she was endowed with fathomless love, pity and a sense of renunciation as well. She had a strange art of consecrating others by her behaviour. That was why, perceptible transformation began to appear in Khande Rao's behaviour. He now began to obey his parents and take active interest in running the kingdom. Malhar Rao was very pleased to see the changes in his son Khande Rao.

Ahilyabai left no stone unturned to win over the heart of her husband. She served him faithfully and made every effort to keep him happy. As Khande Rao's interest grew in state's affairs, Ahilyabai instigated him to master the martial art telling him about the importance of it. Very soon, efforts of Ahilyabai began to pay rich dividends, and Khande Rao began to accompany his father even in the battlefields. Slowly but steadily, he perfected the martial art.

Thus beating all adversities Ahilyabai brought her married life to the right course successfully. After some time, in 1745, she gave birth to a son at a place named Depalpur. A wave of joy swept across the kingdom at the birth of the prince. The son was named Maley Rao. Three years later, in 1748

Ahilyabai gave birth to a girl child. She was named Muktabai.

Golden days of Ahilyabai's happy married life had just begun. With unrelenting hard work, she first transformed her husband and brought him to the righteous course. Her children were yet small. But the cruel destiny could not see even this little happiness of Ahilyabai. Golden rays of pleasure were just appearing in her married life when dark clouds of misfortune suddenly gathered up.

By now Malhar Rao had begun to trust his son's skill of warfare. With an object to train him further, Malhar Rao began to take his son on war expeditions. In 1754, Khande Rao accompanied Malhar Rao when he visited Rajputana to recover *Chauth* (land taxes) alongwith Raghunath Rao Peshwa. They had recovered *Chauth* successfully from most of the principalities of Rajputana. But the king of Bharatpur, Suraj Mal Jat refused outrightly to pay the *Chauth*. When all persuasion failed, Peshwa was forced to declare war. Maratha forces then launched an attack on Khumbher fort near Deeg in the principality of Bharatpur. Jats of Bharatpur too came into the field to counter the attack. A fierce battle set off between Marathas and Jats. On March 24, 1754, riding a horse when Khande Rao was summoning his forces to fight gallantly against the enemy, a bullet fired from the Jat army hit directly in his chest. In no time, Khande Rao attained martyrdom. At that time Malhar Rao was leading the battle in the other part of the fort. He was at once informed about the martyrdom of his son Khande Rao. News of the death of his only son shook Malhar Rao deeply. Tears spurted from his eyes. Commander of Maratha force and the Subedar of Malwa Malhar Rao burst into tears like a child. The war came to a halt instantaneously.

Dead body of Khande Rao was brought to his tent. Ahilyabai was also present there. Her sorrow had no limit when she saw the dead body of her husband. Writhing like a fish

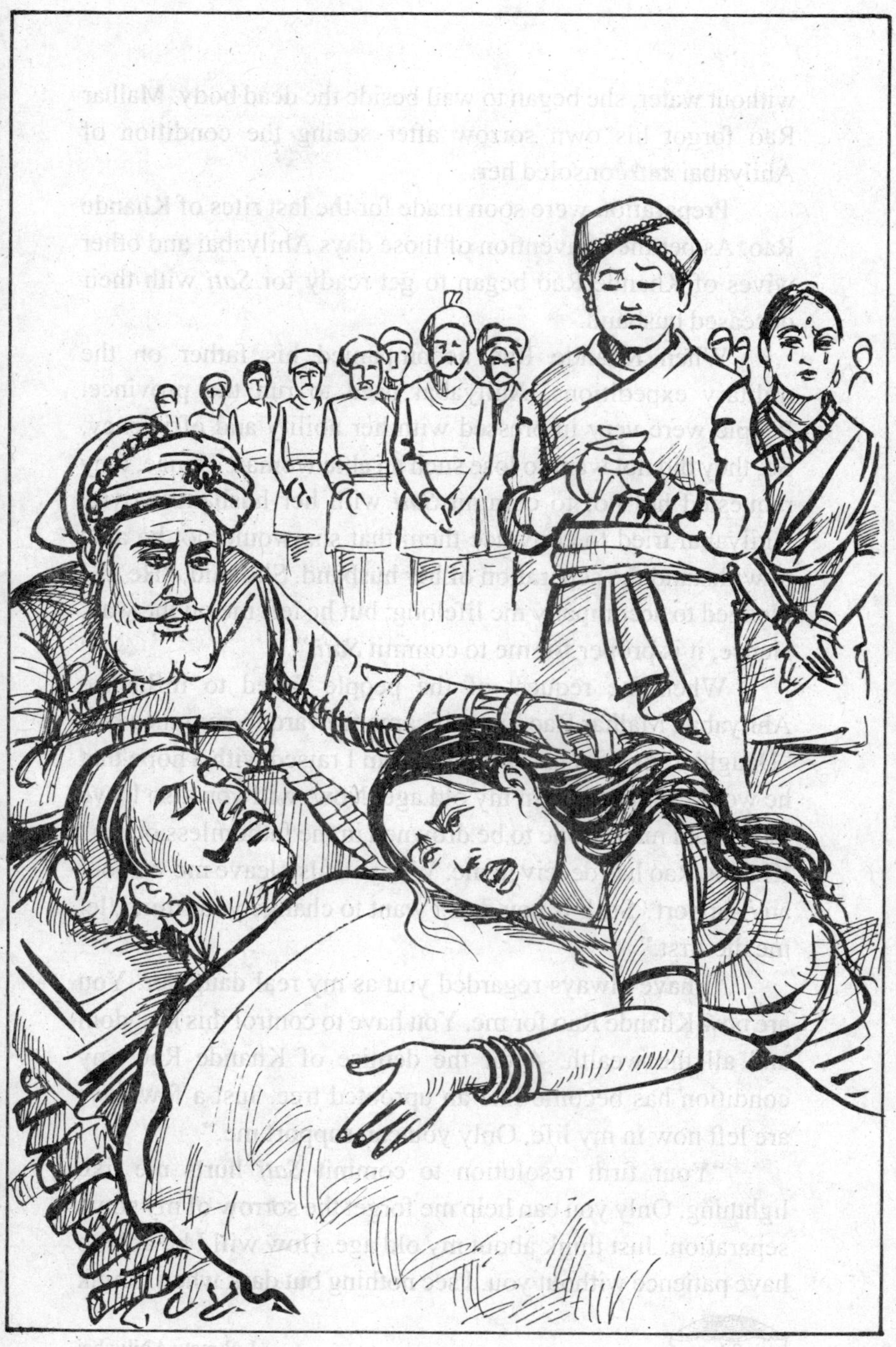

without water, she began to wail beside the dead body. Malhar Rao forgot his own sorrow after seeing the condition of Ahilyabai and consoled her.

Preparation were soon made for the last rites of Khande Rao. As per the convention of those days Ahilyabai and other wives of Khande Rao began to get ready for *Sati* with their deceased husband.

When Khande Rao accompanied his father on the military expeditions, Ahilyabai used to run the province. People were very impressed with her ability and efficiency. So, they did not want to lose such an able woman. Hence, they requested her not to commit *Sati* with her husband's pyre. Ahilyabai tried to convince them that she would not be able to withstand the separation of her husband. She said, "He had pledged to accompany me lifelong; but he left me on the way. Hence, it is proper for me to commit *Sati*."

When the request of the people failed to influence Ahilyabai, Malhar Rao himself came forward to convince her, "Daughter, my son has left me whom I raised with a hope that he would support me in my old age. Now, will you also leave me, an old man, alone to be drowned in the fathomless ocean? Khande Rao has deceived me. Will you also leave me without any support? Still, if you don't want to change your mind, let me die first."

"I have always regarded you as my real daughter. You are now Khande Rao for me. You have to control this kingdom and all the wealth. After the demise of Khande Rao, my condition has become like an uprooted tree. Just a few days are left now in my life. Only you can support me."

"Your firm resolution to commit *Sati* hurts me like lightning. Only you can help me forget the sorrow of my son's separation. Just think about my old age. How will I be able to have patience without you. I see nothing but dark when I think

about you committing *Sati*. Do not speak therefore, O daughter about committing *Sati*, I fall at your feet." Saying these words, Malhar Rao once again burst into tears and fell at Ahilyabai's feet.

Pathetic condition of Malhar Rao was enough to melt even a stone. At last she was forced to give up her hard decision of committing *Sati*.

4
Discharging Duties

After the death of her husband, Ahilyabai took a firm resolution according to the prevailing customs to commit *Sati* alongwith her deceased husband. But for the poignant request by her father-in-law she could not commit *Sati*. Because of the old age of her father-in-law, his continuous involvement in the military expeditions and childhood of her son, duty of running the kingdom fell on her shoulders. Even in the life of Khande Rao this duty had been mostly discharged by Ahilyabai. After his death whole responsibility of the state came to her.

Malhar Rao was fully aware of Ahilyabai's administrative and political abilities and had full faith in her. During emergency periods he used to consult Ahilyabai.

Military expeditions of Malhar Rao continued even after the death of his son. In the battlefield also he used to remain in touch with Ahilyabai through correspondence. Through in the letters, he would often advise Ahilyabai in political matters. Letters sent by Malhar Rao to Ahilyabai contained politics, strategy, diplomacy etc., in detail.

In a letter to Ahilyabai, Malhar Rao says, "You write that stationing of artillery in Gwalior will cause great

mismanagement regarding fodder and water, hence I take artillery to Sirouz. If it is correct, station the artillery in Sirouz and you yourself go to Indore after arranging for the fodder etc., for the oxen in Sirouz. Also make arrangement for the recovery of *Chauth* in Sandhava district and Tajpur. Presently, I am going to Delhi, thence via waterway I will reach Bundelkhand. I will inform you later about the development."

In another letter to Ahilyabai, Malhar Rao says, "Keep in mind the congestion of forces in the fortress while sending artillery towards Gohadkar. Don't take daring action. Get the things done as far as possible by your personal influence; don't send the artillery too far trusting anybody. See that the reputation of artillery is not harmed, while our work at the same time also gets done!"

Contents of these letters reveal that right from the time of Malhar Rao, Ahilyabai had gained enough expertise in politics and warfare. In Malhar Rao's absence she managed the kingdom very well and made arrangements to send fresh ration and military reinforcements for Malhar Rao in the battlefield as well. She also used to lead herself small military expeditions.

In one of his letters to Ahilyabai, Malhar Rao writes, "From the contents of the letter you would have understood the situations here. We have left Delhi and are presently staying in a village Karjoasa near Anoop Shehar. We will celebrate *Holi* here. Najiv is involved in the fight of Gilchiyan. It is a rumour here that Abdali has arrived in Sirhind. Najiv Khan has been sent to him. We will take further action only after he returns with the latest news. Till then, we will camp by the Ganges. After the confirmation of Gilchi, we will move towards Lakurabad. You would have received the letter carried to you by the messenger Deva. Make arrangement for the departure according to the letter. If you are still awaiting for a

trusted man then postpone the departure, don't send anybody towards our side. Stay in Gwalior for the time being, we too will soon reach there, and summon you if the need arises. Messenger has informed us that at the point of your guns you got a fort vacated in Gohad. So, stay in Gwalior for the moment and open the factories of artilleries and ammunitions in Zamburn to produce warheads in ample quantity. It is necessary for us to defeat the occupants of Gohad. Send the ration through a trusted man, otherwise let it remain there."

In one more letter, Malhar Rao writes, "Keep writing about you. We had written you to send the ration. We have heard that all of you are planning to come here. You know about our desire. How fair would it be for you to come here without our permission. Should you need our permission, send the ration through Rajeshri Bahero Anand or Rajeshri Govind Shamrao and go yourself to Sirouz. We do not need Maley Rao or anybody else here. So do as directed keeping this in mind. Abdali has reached Sirhind. Shujauddaulah and all other Rohillas have united. Gilchi is about to arrive in Delhi. We will do as the situation warrants us in future. Without wasting even a moment you migrate to Sirouz without taking the artillery and don't make a halt anywhere on the way. Send the ration via Batishwar as per our instruction."

Thus, in the letter, worried by the adverse conditions at the front, Malhar Rao instructs Ahilyabai not to come to the front and make arrangement staying back in Sirouz and send the ration and other warheads. In yet another letter, Malhar Rao writes to his daughter-in-law Ahilyabai, "We are safe here. Write about you. Tanu has taken the artillery to you. You keep this artillery to Sirouz and move ahead making arrangement for the fodder etc. for the oxen. Instruct Rajeshri Chimanji Govind Mamaledar for the necessary repair of the guns to keep them ready. Don't allow any carelessness. We will soon be

reaching there and we will need the guns there. We must find the guns ready. Take care of the ropes etc., and keep them ready right tomorrow, keep the oxen also ready. Tanu has also written for the readiness of the guns. You instruct your man to make proper arrangement of the oxen etc."

All these letters had been written in a single year which show the conditions that prevailed during those days. Having engaged for the war preparations at the front near Delhi, Malhar Rao continued to remain in touch with Ahilyabai and guiding her in politics and instructing her for the manufacture of warheads. Staying at Malwa, Ahilyabai not only properly looked after the management of the state with superb efficiency but also made every arrangement of the production of the warheads and ration and sent them readily to her father-in-law at the front. She even led many smaller war fronts successfully.

These letters also reveal how much expertise Ahilyabai had gained during her initial years in discharging her political responsibilities and helped her father-in-law who was constantly engaged in wars at the front.

5
Death of Father-in-law

Malhar Rao was very dejected at the untimely death of his son Khande Rao. The cruel blow of destiny had shaken him in his old age. His mind was pinning for peace and retirement in the last stage of his life, but political circumstances were reluctant to allow him any rest. Atmosphere of disturbance and uncertainty prevailed all around the country. Hence despite his fervent desire, rest was not possible for him. Moreover, there was a strong urge in his mind to avenge the death of his son. Hence, despite a heavy burden of sorrow in his mind, Malhar Rao engaged himself constantly in war expeditions.

Reputation of Marathas had suffered a serious setback in the country after their defeat by Ahmed Shah Abdali in the battle of Panipat in 1761. Smaller kings and chieftains had begun to rise in rebellion here and there throughout the country. Even many local landlords, whose vested interests had been affected by the establishment of Maratha empire in Malwa began to raise their heads taking full advantage of the opportunity.

Thus, in the prevailing condition of political turmoil, it was not possible for Malhar Rao to take the least rest. But working unrelentingly with superb political understanding, Malhar Rao managed to curb all the adverse circumstances in a short span of time and re-established his rule in Malwa. No one but Malhar Rao could have achieved this feat. Peshwa exalted Malhar Rao lavishly for his success and honoured him by granting the right to rule entire northern India along with Malwa.

Later, Maratha forces once again launched an attack on northern India with an object of compensating for the losses they had incurred because of their defeat in Panipat battle. Raghoba Peshwa was leading the Maratha forces, that included among others, Mahadji Sindhia, Malhar Rao Holkar, Tukoji Rao and Maley Rao. Marathas had to work hard to defeat the king of Gohad. Though the king of Gohad had been defeated, but the severe exertion had left old Malhar Rao in an exhausted state. He fell ill. Injury that he had received in Mangrol battle became an incurable wound. For a little rest, his army camped in Alampur. Malhar Rao was having unbearable pain in his ear. All treatments failed to relieve his pain that grew continuously. His end had come. Hope of avenging the death of his son had remained dormant in his heart. He was specially sorry for it. Mahadji Sindhia, Tukoji Rao and Maley Rao were standing beside him. Calling Maley Rao near him, Malhar Rao said, "Now, in my place, you will serve Shrimant Peshwa." Then, handing Maley Rao over to Tukoji Rao, he made him the guardian of Maley Rao. Thus, on May 30, 1766, Malhar Rao breathed his last in Alampur at an age of 73.

Death of her father-in-law Malhar Rao was a serious blow to Ahilyabai. Malhar Rao was not just a father-in-law; he was also an affectionate father, knowledgeable teacher as well as a political guide to Ahilyabai. With his death, Ahilyabai had lost a protection cover.

Gloomily, with heavy heart, Ahilyabai arranged for the

last rites of her father-in-law and got a canopy built in Alampur in his memory. She also made permanent arrangement for the maintenance of the canopy as well.

Malhar Rao was a great and gallant commander of his time. He was born in 1693 in an ordinary shepherd family. But with his dutifulness and ability, he reached the post of Subedar of Malwa province. His bravery held the sway in the entire northern India. All important people from Shrimant Peshwa to the emperor of Delhi tried to keep him pleased. He had an important role in the expansion of Maratha empire in northern India. He was an intimate friend of Peshwa and the pedestal of the Maratha empire.

Malhar Rao was an excellent warrior and equestrian. His whole life passed in riding horses and fighting great battles. He was an expert in archery and fencing, yet lance was his favourite weapon. He used to respect bravery very much and filled the shields of those soldiers with money who showed exceptional bravery. Even the minister of the enemy kingdoms exalted his bravery liberally.

Courtier bard of Suraj Mal Jat, *Mahakavi* Sudama has praised Malhar Rao in his work *Sujan Charit*:

Hare Dekhi Hada Manamare Kama Dhuj Bansa
Koomar Pasor Payn Sunat Nagare Ke!
Kete Pur Jare Kete Nripati San Mare
Tei Jori Dala Bhare Braj Bhumi Pe Hankare Ke!

(Whose fear sets tremors even in great Rajput kings, such a dignified King Malhar Rao came with a huge army to invade Brajbhumi setting many towns on fire and killing many kings on the way.)

These lines described the time when Malhar Rao had launched an attack on Suraj Mal Jat, the king of Bharatpur. This exaltation of Malhar Rao by the courtier poet of Suraj

Mal shows, how strong an influence did Malhar Rao enjoy in entire northern India.

Another poet, Khushali Ram writes:

Vero Mahan Yodh Ganeshu Mukh Yo
Baladhipah Shastra Vidhan Sugyan!
Sada Yashasvi Satat Samartho
Malhari Rao Vadi Tah Prithiv Yam!!

(He, who is known on the earth as Malhar Rao, is the great among the gallant warriors, leader of the strong ones, skilled in warfare, able, always active and reputed.)

Malhar Rao is said to be the founder of the modern Indore city. Before he founded Indore, it was a small hamlet. Malhar Rao made the hamlet his capital and got a huge principality built on the bank of the river Kauh, and started to build a planned dwelling at Indore. He offered many incentives and facilities to the traders, businessmen and artisans to establish their businesses in Indore. Thus, Malhar Rao is an extremely important name in the history of Indore.

6
Separation from Son

Despite the birth in an ordinary family Ahilyabai had become the daughter-in-law of a royal family, but it was not in her fate to enjoy the royal pleasures. Pleasures were a faraway dream. Even a peaceful mind, free of worries was not in her fate. During the initial years of her married life misconduct of her husband Khande Rao was her main worry. Somehow she managed to reform him and brought him to the righteous course. But then, he met tragic death in the battle of Khumbher. Ahilyabai was forced to give up her resolution of committing *Sati* with her dead husband just to serve her old father-in-law and discharge the serious duty of administering the kingdom. But again, within a few years she lost her caring father-in-law also. Now, all her hopes came to rest on her only son Maley Rao. But here too destiny was getting ready to fail her once again.

Maley Rao was endowed with all kinds of elements that the uncultured children of a prosperous family have. Despite all her political engagements, Ahilyabai left no stone unturned to inculcate culture in her son. But she could not get even the least success in her efforts of transforming her son. Fickle minded and aggressive Maley Rao had no interest in studies.

Wandering like a vagabond all the day long in a troupe of vagrant boys was his daily routine. He was fond of bathing in the river and watching the water plays of elephants. He had diabolical demonic hobbies of hiding scorpions in the shoes of his teachers and the priests, who came to teach him and carry out worship, and enjoyed watching them writhing in pain when the scorpions bit them. Ahilyabai tried convincing and even gave punishment to reform her son, but she could not succeed even the least bit in her efforts.

After the death of Malhar Rao, coronation of Maley Rao was carried out on August 23, 1766, and he was appointed formally as the Subedar of Malwa by Peshwa. But the real powers to run the kingdom were vested in the hands of Ahilyabai because Peshwa was fully aware of the inability of Maley Rao. Ahilyabai had thought that the burden of responsibilities would induce seriousness in Maley Rao, but it did not happen. Already arrogant Maley Rao became even more unruly when he got powers. His conditions made Ahilyabai even more worried. She loved her subjects too much and always worked for their welfare. She firmly believed the interest of the subjects is the interest of the king. Welfare of king is dependent upon the pleasure of the subjects. She expected her son Maley Rao also to follow her righteous course but her expectation never materialized. Maley Rao did not show expected reforms.

Ahilyabai always tried to convince her son Maley Rao that he should strive to achieve the same level of greatness that his grandfather had achieved; then only his life would become meaningful.

In a letter to Maley Rao from Charoli, Ahilyabai writes, "I feel unrest for not receiving a letter from you. Don't do that, keep writing about you. I have written two or three letters to you. Try to pacify your mind and don't mourn. Be

considerate about your *Subedari* and run the kingdom. You should also run the kingdom as prudently as it had once been run by your late grandfather, shed the sadness and run the kingdom with farsightedness to earn even greater fame than your grandfather. Your pride lies in it. Behave as per the desire of Rajeshri Gangadhar Pant Tatya."

It is clear from the letter that Ahilyabai constantly worried about the fame of her lineage, duty and the welfare of her kingdom. Hence, again and again in her letters she cautioned her son about his duties. Hence, in this letter, she suggested her son to act according to the desire of her Diwan Gangadhar Pant.

But despite all efforts by Ahilyabai, Maley Rao did not change his bad habits. His imprudence grew constantly and he tortured his subjects in ever increasing manner. Complaints against his action fell in the ears of his mother also, but she had to contain herself. She prayed to God to change the behaviour of her son, vowed to make offerings and observed fasts also. But Maley Rao's conduct did not change at all, and he continued to receive the curses of the victims.

Once, misguided by someone, Maley Rao killed an innocent person. Later on, when he came to know about the reality, he fell seriously ill because of guilt feeling. Great efforts were made for his treatment, but he could not be cured. Everything from prayers and recitation, talismans and witchcraft, magic and sorcery, herbs and medicine were tried, but his illness continued to grow. Ahilyabai made hard efforts to save the life of her son, but all in vain. After ruling for only nine months, Maley Rao too left this mortal world at a raw age of twenty-two. After his death, his two wives too committed *Sati* on his pyre.

Sorrow of Ahilyabai knew no limit in the separation of her only son. After all, Maley Rao was her only son, and there

is no mother who would not be moved by the death of her only son. For a moment a strong sense of detachment overpowered her. Renouncing everything, she took a resolution to pass her remaining life in a place of pilgrimage and praying to God. But in the next moment, prudence controlled her mind once again. Consideration of the same subjects once more compelled her to swallow the bitter potion of the separation of her only son. Duty still came first to her, and bearing all agony of her son's death, Ahilyabai assumed the role of *Lokmata* and dedicated herself to remove the miseries of her subjects.

In the memory of her son she got a beautiful canopy built in Indore.

About the death of Maley Rao, a hearsay is popular among the people that because of his misconduct and atrocities, Ahilyabai got her son trampled under the feet of the elephants. But the historical evidences do not support this hearsay. Many people believe this. In any case, the hearsay proves, beyond all doubts, that Lokmata Ahilyabai loved her subjects more than her son. And the people had such a strong faith in the piety and justice of Ahilyabai that they gave more importance to their faith and trust than any historical fact.

7
Humiliation of Raghoba

Maley Rao had no son. So, the issue of his successor arose after his death. Subjects of Holkar Kingdom wanted to see Devi Ahilya control reigns of the state because for the past many years she had been actually running the kingdom with great efficiency and piety irrespective of the occupant of *Subedari*. During the time of Malhar Rao, Ahilyabai used to run the kingdom because Malhar Rao would stay away in the war front. After the death of Malhar Rao, Ahilyabai continued to look after the administration under the guidance of Peshwa because Maley Rao was a minor at that time. It was natural then, that in the changed circumstances the subjects wanted her to rule the state. But it was unacceptable to many men of the state to see a helpless widow occupying the throne of the kingdom. It even appeared to them against the scriptures. Diwan of the kingdom Gangadhar Yashwant Chandrachur too had the same opinion. He was one of the trusted companions of late Malhar Rao. He had come to Indore with Malhar Rao and played an important role in the administration of the Holkar Kingdom right from the beginning. Even Devi Ahilya respected his ability. In one of her letters she had even suggested Maley Rao to follow the advice of Gangadhar Pant. But in the changed

scenario even Gangadhar Pant, who was once loyal to Devi Ahilya, went against her. Gangadhar Pant advised Devi Ahilya to adopt a son who could be enthroned as the new *Subedar*.

By that time, Devi Ahilya had gained sufficient political maturity. She did not take long to sense the shrewd diplomacy hidden behind the seemingly innocent advice of Gangadhar Pant. She knew well that enthronement of a minor as *Subedar* would require her to surrender all her administrative powers. Then, whole administration would go into the hands of Gangadhar Pant.

Devi Ahilya had a firm belief that the king is for the safety of the subjects. A king who fails to satisfy his subjects, ultimately goes to hell. She understood that the enthronement of a minor boy would mean transfer of administrative powers into the hands of the officials, who would then plunder the subjects freely in the absence of an effective control. Hence, she rejected outright the suggestion of adopting a minor boy and his enthronement as the Subedar.

She said, "I am the daughter-in-law, wife and the mother respectively of the people who have ruled this state. It is, therefore, not only my inherent right, but a duty also that I must take the administration of the kingdom in my hands in this difficult situation and discharge my responsibility of removing the miseries of the subjects."

This determination of Devi Ahilya infuriated Gangadhar Pant and his colleagues. They said, "How can an orphan, widow rule the kingdom in our presence. It is daring for a frail woman to challenge diplomats like us." Thus they resolved to make arbitrary arrangement for the state smashing the self-respect of a feeble woman.

Diwan Gangadhar Pant then informed Raghunath Rao Peshwa through a letter that after the death of issueless Maley Rao, the kingdom had no legitimate successor. "Hence, come

with a strong force and capture the kingdom." Raghunath Rao, also known as Raghoba, was himself hungry for power, why would he waste the opportunity. So, at once he directed his forces towards Indore.

Diwan Gangadhar Pant Chandrachur had committed a mistake in underestimating the strength of Devi Ahilya. When a seemingly frail woman takes a firm resolution, she can humiliate even the strongest man. Spies of Devi Ahilya had been informing her about the vicious moves of Diwan Gangadhar Pant and his associates. She had already got the information about the letter written secretly by Gangadhar Pant to Raghoba. She also came to know that Raghoba had started for Indore with his fifty thousand strong army.

An ordinary woman would have been taken by surprise at these developments, and in all probability she would have bowed before the plan of Gangadhar Pant. But Devi Ahilya had exceptional courage. It was not her nature to concede defeat before the circumstances. She at once resolved to destroy the vicious plans of Gangadhar Pant and Raghoba. In a roaring voice, she said, "No one should take me for granted, that I am a woman, a frail woman and widow, and hence they can suppress me easily; I will be invincible for anybody if I come to stand in the battlefield taking my lance. We are the Subedar of Peshwa, and always ready to serve him. But it would not be possible for anybody to usurp the Holkar Kingdom in all the three ages. My father-in-law had not acquired this kingdom by flattery. He won it by the strength of his sword. We will not spare the life of anybody who dares to eye our kingdom menacingly."

Summoning her trusted men then, Devi Ahilya took stock of her powers and declared to take over the reigns of the state administration in her hands. A wave of enthusiasm ran across among the public when they heard about Devi Ahilya's

declaration of taking over the controls of the state. People knew that Devi Ahilya was an unselfish, altruist, just and religious ruler and she had taken over the administration of the state realizing her duty for the benefit of her subjects.

Devi Ahilya then intimated her commander-in-chief Tukoji Rao about the situation and instructed him to arrive in Indore at once for the safety of the kingdom. She then sent letters to Mahadji Sindhia, Bhosale, Gaikwar, Dabhare and other commanders and informed them about the emergency that was facing her, reminding them of the services, and assistance rendered to them by her father-in-law late Malhar Rao and requested them to come forward for the help of the Holkar Kingdom at that difficult time. In reply, all the commanders expressed their indebtedness to late Malhar Rao and assured her of their fullest co-operation.

In a letter to Shrimant Madhav Rao Peshwa, Devi Ahilya intimated him about the conspiracy that Gangadhar Pant had hatched with Raghoba to usurp her kingdom. Madhav Rao Peshwa was himself a just and pious ruler. He knew the mentality of his uncle very well. In reply to Ahilyabai, he wrote, "Should someone launch an attack to usurp your kingdom, stand against him and drive him away. To rule the Holkar Kingdom is your right. Be assured from our side."

Thus forming such strategy, Devi Ahilya arranged an army of women with a numerical strength of five hundred. She trained the army and armed it with different kinds of weapons. She also collected necessary ammunition and ration and handed them over to the army.

Just then, news came that Raghoba had arrived in Ujjain and camped on the bank of Kshipra with his fifty thousand strong forces. He was also awaiting for the arrival of the forces of Sindhia, Gaikwar, Dabhare etc., whom he had ordered through letters to come for his help. But all of them plainly refused to fight against Ahilyabai on his behalf. Not only that, their forces arrived there to help Ahilyabai. Receiving the blessings of Devi Ahilya, commander-in-chief Tukoji Rao too had arrived on the banks of Kshipra. In a message Tukoji Rao cautioned Raghoba that if he crossed Kshipra with an intention of attacking, their swords would be drawn out to counter him.

Meanwhile, Raghoba received a letter from Ahilyabai, in which she had written, "You have come here with an evil intention of usurping my kingdom. You think that I am a weak woman. But your intention shall never materialize. But you will come to know my strength in the battlefield. I will counter you with my women forces. Nobody will deride me if I lose, but nobody will praise your victory either. But if you lose, you will never be able to show your face anywhere. Blemish of attacking a weak woman can never be wiped out. Consider all these things in detail before entering the battlefield."

This straightforward letter of Devi Ahilya slackened the fervour of Raghoba. He had already become aware of the war preparations of Devi Ahilya, hence he saw his benefit in not fighting against her. At once changing his stratagem he despatched a letter to Tukoji Rao that "you are misunderstanding us that we have come to attack the Holkar Kingdom. Considering our past relations with late Malhar Rao, we can not even imagine to fight against his daughter-in-law. We have, in fact, come to express our condolences at the death of late Maley Rao, the son of Devi Ahilya."

Tukoji Rao at once sent a reply, "You were not required to come with such a huge army just to show you condolences. Leave the forces there, and come with us to Indore, we will accord you full honour." Raghoba had lost the move. He was left with no option but to accept Tukoji Rao's proposal. So he left his army back on the bank of Kshipra and accompanied by his wife and some commanders came riding a palanquin to

the camp of Tukoji Rao. With full respect Tukoji Rao greeted him and escorted him to Indore. In Indore, Devi Ahilya gave Raghoba a traditional warm welcome. Devi Ahilya and Raghoba held lengthy discussion, but they had obliterated the bitter events that occurred only a few days ago. Raghoba stayed in Indore for about a month. During that period, Raghoba came to know about Devi Ahilya and was fully impressed by her personality. He did not discuss the issue of adopting successor again. At last, parting with Devi, he took off the camps of his army and returned to Poona. Ashamed of his action Gangadhar Chandrachur too went to Poona in the name of a pilgrimage.

Thus, Devi Ahilya took firm hold of the administration of the state. She faced the crisis that had threatened the existence of her kingdom with bravery and cleverness and protected the kingdom from all sides. This incidence led to an increased reputation of Devi Ahilya's ability and wisdom. A sense of cheerfulness and enthusiasm prevailed among her subjects.

8
Maheshwar: The New Capital

After the death of her only son Maley Rao, Devi Ahilya's mind had become totally averse to mundane matters. One by one, her husband, father-in-law and son had left her. Now, life appeared completely worthless to her. Many a times a strong urge would appear in her mind to renounce everything and go to stay in a place of pilgrimage and pass her remaining life in the devotion of the Lord. But the pledge she had once made to her father-in-law, late Malhar Rao to look after the kingdom plus the worry of her subjects stymied her from renouncing everything. She was in a strange state. She had only one worry—how to achieve a balance between the welfare of her subjects and her own summom bonum. At last she did find a way out.

She had a great reverence for the sacred Narmada river. Narmada was not too far from Indore. There were many holy places of pilgrimage along the bank of Narmada. Devi Ahilya decided to shift her capital to one such place of pilgrimage on the bank of Narmada, where she could run her kingdom as well as train her salvation.

With this view Ahilyabai carried out survey of the villages situated along the bank of Narmada. A village named

Mardana in Nimar district appeared as the most suitable place for founding her capital. But the astrologers told her that the village was not fit for making it the capital, so she dropped the idea of making her capital in Mardana. Then her attention was drawn to Maheshwar. Maheshwar appeared to her as an optimum place for making the capital as well as satiating her religious urge.

Founding of the capital by Devi Ahilya in Maheshwar proved fortunate for that place. Devi Ahilya passed about twenty-eight years of her remaining life in Maheshwar. During this period, Maheshwar appeared in prominence on the map of the country as an important centre. Ambassadors, politicians, savants, sages and ascetics from all the prominent provinces of the country used to visit Maheshwar regularly. This led to all round development of Maheshwar and this ancient pilgrimage town once again came to be reckoned among the prominent cities of India.

Renowned in ancient India as Avantika and Mahishmati, respectively, Ujjain of Malwa and Maheshwar of Nimar are the two prominent places of pilgrimage with great historical significance situated near Indore. Both these cities have great archaeological importance, and find mention in the scriptures of Jain and Buddhist besides great epics like *Ramayana* and *Mahabharata* and many *Puranas*. Since, Maheshwar was situated within the Holkar Kingdom, Devi Ahilya selected this place to build her capital. It had been a prosperous and flourishing city during the ages of *Ramayana* and *Mahabharata* also. Evidences show that Arjuna had arrived here during his mission of universal conquest.

This city had been founded by a king Mahishmana. Many kings, who were renowned in *Puranas* and history, had a relation with this city. The same Mahishmati was the capital of the King Sahastrarjun's kingdom Anupdesh. Great poet

Kalidas had mentioned this city in his famous work *Meghdoot*. Famous debate between Adi Shankaracharya and popular Sanskrit scholar savant Mandan Mishra had taken place here. During the time of Hahaya Chalukya and Paramar kings, this city had special significance. It had been included, in later periods, into the kingdoms of Sultans of Mandav and Gujarat. And before inclusion into the Holkar Kingdom, Maheshwar was in Mughal occupation. In 1730, Malhar Rao Holkar snatched Malwa and Nimar from the Mughals and established Holkar Kingdom. Since then Maheshwar had been in Holkar Kingdom.

Appreciating the significance of this city, Malhar Rao had issued a special edict in 1745, in which he declared many facilities for the weavers, carpenters, labourers and the traders and ordered them to settle in Maheshwar and contribute in its all round development.

Maheshwar is situated on the bank of Narmada river. Narmada is one of India's seven most prominent and sacred rivers. It is the only river in the world which is circumambulated by thousands of devotees every year. Devi Ahilya too had strong faith and reverence for Narmada. Thus, she built her capital in Maheshwar and spent a major part of her life near the bank of Narmada. In Maheshwar, Ahilyabai got the renovation of many old temples done, which were on the verge of ruins. She also got many new temples and jetties as well as many houses built for the savants, Brahmins and weavers.

Maheshwar had already had a great geographical significance due to its location on the trunk road joining north and south India. After becoming the capital of Devi Ahilya's kingdom, its political, social as well as commercial importance also grew significantly. Devi Ahilya invited respectfully selected savants, religious teachers, astrologers, puranics, psalmists, artists and artisans from all over the country and

helped them to settle in Maheshwar. She also got many Sanskrit schools started. Tradition of regular worship and other religious ceremonies in the temples also began in her time. To conduct these functions, hundreds of Brahmins and priests also settled in Maheshwar. Recitation of hymns and musical sounds of songs, conchs and other instruments reverberated all the day long in the temples of Maheshwar. Devi Ahilya opened her treasure to make donations to the Brahmins and the poors and to feed them public kitchens used to be run by her aid. Delegations, ambassadors and cousellors from different kingdoms also used to visit Maheshwar regularly to meet Devi Ahilya.

Devi Ahilya also got the construction of temples, jetties, inns, canopies etc., done in almost all the places of pilgrimage in the entire country. Construction of these structures required thousands of artisans and masons. Thousands of sculptors, statuaries, artisans etc., who were searching employment, came to settle in Maheshwar.

Efforts of Devi Ahilya led to the establishment of Maheshwar as a prominent centre of cloth industry on the commercial map of the country. She invited the skilled weavers from all parts of the country and helped them to settle in Maheshwar. She helped them financially to start their business; she also bought *sarees* and other goods produced by those weavers to encourage them. Because of her inspiration and incentives, high quality *sarees* and clothes began to be produced in Maheshwar. These products had exquisite artistic work also. Devi Ahilya herself used to wear *sarees* manufactured in Maheshwar and presented her guests with the clothes made in Maheshwar, as gifts. Business of the weavers began to flourish because of the liberal support, high taste and incentives of Devi Ahilya and the artisans also grew in prosperity.

Contemporary poet and singer of Maharashtra—Anant Fandi writes about Maheshwar, "Maheshwar is situated on the bank of Narmada. It has huge jetties and high rising temples. Narmada is very deep there, hence the city appears as beautiful and pleasing as Kailash. Houses and mansions are gorgeous. Reputation of Ahilyabai brings people to Maheshwar and they are obliged by her liberal grants. Maheshwar has immense wealth, city bustles with life. It has big markets, big shops and millionaire businessmen. Shops have all kinds of goods, goods are cheap and there is no shortage of any thing. Ahilyabai fosters her subjects like her own children. She takes full care of their safety and comfort. She has pledged to distribute free food daily through the public kitchens for the poors. Poors, savants as well as sages and saints from all over the country visit Maheshwar; Devi donates them liberally. Daily she worships Lord Shiva and makes donations."

From the description, it becomes clear that how a small, ordinary town Maheshwar transformed into a flourishing city by the efforts of Devi Ahilya. Being the capital of Holkar Kingdom, many kings sent their representatives to stay permanently in Maheshwar. These representatives had been housed in gorgeous mansions. Many big businessmen too had their mansions in Maheshwar. A curiosity, therefore, arises naturally in mind about the palace of Devi Ahilya who was the owner of that rich city. The residence of Devi Ahilya was not as huge and gorgeous as those of the other businessmen and ambassadors had been. Her residence could aptly be called a hermitage. It was a small, simple, two storeyed house, such as owned by some middle class person. It appeared more like a temple or place of pilgrimage, having a divinely tranquil ambience. In this same, penancing hut like house, Devi Ahilya held parleys with the great kings and their messengers; met her ministers, chieftains, politicians and subjects and took decisions of the national importance. In one of the rooms, Devi had fenced off some place for worship, where every morning she used to pray and worship God. In the courtyard of the house, there was a small basil-grove, and in front of the house was the huge jetty of Narmada, where Devi used to take her bath. Near the house there was a small garden in which flowers and basil plants had been grown for the purpose of worship.

Like the great life of Devi Ahilya, her simple residence was also a centre of inspiration and reverence for the people. It is still maintained in the same state as it used to be at the time of Devi Ahilya. Thousands of people from all over the world visit Maheshwar to pay their tribute to Devi Ahilya even today. When they return they take great inspiration from her brilliant life and works with them. After watching this simple residence of Devi Ahilya and while presiding over the function of Devi Ahilya National Award ceremony in Indore, Governor of Madhya Pradesh, His Highness Dr. Bhai Mahaveer said in his speech, "People, particularly the politicians must visit Maheshwar and see the simple but extraordinary residence of Devi Ahilya. Only then, they will realize that how, despite being the owner of a huge and prosperous kingdom, the pious Devi Ahilya spent her life like an expiator. Having seen her lifestyle, the modern politicians will be ashamed of their luxurious life."

After the demise of Devi Ahilya, Maharaja Yashwant Rao I got a huge canopy and many jetties built in Maheshwar. All of them are beautiful and worth seeing. Canopy cum cenotaph of Devi Ahilya took thirty-four years and a cost of about one and a half crore rupees in its construction.

9

Marriage of Daughter

Devi Ahilya had two offsprings, a son Maley Rao and a daughter Muktabai. After the demise of her mother and father-in-law, husband and son, only Muktabai was left with her. Naturally, she was very dear to her. Now, she had grown up and Devi Ahilya was searching a suitable groom for her. So far, Devi Ahilya could not make sincere effort for the marriage of Muktabai because of political uncertainty and crises in the family.

After Devi Ahilya took the control of the kingdom in her hands and shifted the capital to Maheshwar, she gave the administrative reforms top priority. Administration of the state was in total disarray due to political uncertainties, law and order had deteriorated and the terror of thieves and robbers was rampant. People worked in constant fear. To recover her subjects from the terror, Devi Ahilya resolved to exterminate the thieves and robbers strengthening law and order. She summoned all the prominent chieftains, officials, soldiers and citizens to her court and held a discussion on this subject in a crowded court. Invoking them to exterminate the robbers from the state, she declared in the court—"Whoever exterminate the robbers in the state and relieves my subjects from their

fear, I will marry my only daughter to him."

In those days, caste and creed, high and low status, poverty and richness etc., played an all important role in settling marriages. But Devi Ahilya had declared to marry her only daughter to such a brave man who would curb and exterminate the bandits in the kingdom. Thus, she gave more weightage to gallantry than birth or clan, as a criterion of selecting the groom for her only daughter. She regarded bravery as the greatest merit, rising above the levels of caste and creed, high and low status, poverty and richness etc., thus putting her only daughter on stake and presented the supreme example of renunciation and dedication for the benefit of her subjects.

The whole court stood in silence after hearing the declaration of Devi Ahilya. For a while, nobody came forward to accept the challenge. People began to think that the kingdom had no courageous person, who could face the bandits. Suddenly, a young man named Yashwant Rao Fanase got up. Bravely he accepted the challenge, but put a condition to be provided with all necessary forces and money to carry out the operation. Silently praising the young man, Devi Ahilya provided him with all the necessary forces and money.

Yashwant Fanase was an intelligent and courageous man. In a short time, acting with courage, he wiped out the terror of the thieves and bandits and reinstated peace in the kingdom. It is an eternal truth that a thing earned with hard work appears dearer than something received easily. Yashwant Rao Fanase exterminated the thieves and robbers with his unrelenting hard work and thus showing his courage passed the criterion of Devi. Thus, he had proved his suitability as the fittest groom for the beloved daughter of Devi Ahilya. Keeping her pledge, Devi Ahilya married her daughter Muktabai to Yashwant Rao Fanase. All the citizens of Maheshwar had been invited on the occasion. They were fed with delicious food, and presented

with clothes and cash donations to their satisfaction. Devi presented gold ornaments and *Tarana Pargana* to her daughter as dowry. Thus, instructing Muktabai about the norms of married life, Devi Ahilya saw her off.

10
Suppression of the Revolt

Devi Ahilya had just succeeded in exterminating the thieves, bandits and the brigands and reinstated peace and law and order in the kingdom, when the clouds of revolt began to gather up in the bordering areas of her kingdom. Holkar Kingdom had a common border with the Rampura Pargana of Rajasthan. That region was inhabited by Chandravat Rajputs, who were related to Rana clans of Udaipur. History of their inclusion in the Holkar Kingdom was not an old one.

King of Jaipur, Sawai Jai Singh had two sons—Madhav Singh and Ishwari Singh. After Jai Singh, a struggle began between them for power. Madhav Singh was then living with his Chandravanshi maternal uncle Rana Sangram Singh in Udaipur. Sangram Singh had given Madhav Singh some areas for sustenance. In the absence of Madhav Singh, Ishwari Singh occupied the throne in Jaipur. This led to a power struggle between the two brothers. Madhav Singh's cousin, and king of Udaipur wanted to enthrone him in Jaipur. But he lacked the power to defeat Ishwari Singh. Hence, they had sought the help of Malhar Rao to obtain their ruling right. Accepting the just right of Madhav Singh, Malhar Rao ensured him of all possible assistance and wrote to Ishwari Singh instructing him

to surrender the throne to his brother Madhav Singh or face the war. For the fear of Malhar Rao, Ishwari Singh committed suicide, and thus Madhav Singh got his rights. As a thanksgiving, Madhav Singh presented Malhar Rao with sixty-four lakh rupees plus the area of Rampura that his uncle had given him.

Cousin of Madhav Singh did not like this action that without his permission he gave a part of Chandravat's kingdom to Marathas. But for the dominance of Malhar Rao, they could not oppose him then. After the death of Malhar Rao, however, Chandravats of Rampura used to rise in rebellion occasionally to get freedom from Holkar domination. But every time, Devi Ahilya used to suppress their revolt by immediately sending a force there. Since Chandravats had no support from other Rajput kings of Rajasthan, hence their revolt could never succeed. Rajput kings of Rajasthan were afraid of the power of the Holkar Kingdom; moreover a huge army of Mahadji Sindhia had been stationed in Rajasthan. Because of the combined strength of Holkar and Sindhia, Rajput kings hesitated to openly support the revolt of Chandravats.

But the fire of discontent had been smouldering in the hearts of Rajputs against Marathas. They had been awaiting for the right opportunity, when suddenly they got a golden chance by their sheer luck. Mahadji Sindhia had been defeated in the battle of Lalsote. Consequently his forces had fled from Rajasthan and the hold of the Marathas grew weaker in Rajputana. Taking full advantage of the opportunity, Rajput powers began to unite against the Marathas. Very soon the smouldering fire of discontent turned into blazing flares ready to scorch the Maratha power.

All this development fanned up the courage of Chandravats in Rampura also. They too began to thrash their limbs to be free from Holkar dominations. As a result, dense, formidable clouds of war began to gather up on the border of Holkar Kingdom. Rajput swords began to brandish, eager to uproot and throw out Maratha power.

This time, when Chandravats had risen up in revolt, Devi Ahilya's commander-in-chief Subedar Tukoji Rao was away in far south leading a war expedition. Chandravats had anticipated that in the absence of Tukoji Rao, Devi Ahilya would not be able to face them, and they would get an easy victory. But they were wrong. They did not know Devi Ahilya well, who had full knowledge of their movements and who had already prepared an action plan to deal with them. She had already instructed her all the chieftains to keep the forces prepared. She herself had prepared her army and had been arranging for the ration, ammunition, explosives etc. Associate Maratha chieftains and Shrimant Peshwa in Poona too had been intimated about the development. While Devi Ahilya was busy in war preparations, Shivaji Nana, incharge of Nimbahera fortress, which was situated in Rampura Pargana, arrived. He had fled deserting the fortress. Shivaji Nana told Ahilyabai that there were only one hundred Maratha soldiers in the fortress and two thousand Rajput soldiers had attacked the fortress, "Hence I deserted the fortress." Shivaji Nana also informed that the forces of Udaipur's Rana had invaded the Holkar Kingdom upto Chakharda, and Jagirdar Chandravat of Rampura had joined the rebels against the domination of Holkar.

Words of Shivaji Nana infuriated Devi Ahilya. Roaring with anger she said, "Shivaji Nana, fleeing from the fortress instead of countering the enemies, you have shown great cowardice. You would have attained heaven, had you died confronting the enemies instead of fleeing. And if you had any fear that Ahilyabai would get you decapitated, you would not have dared to run away. Your behaviour has only added to

the courage of the enemy. Now they are attacking us with double enthusiasm. It is all an outcome of your blunder."

Just then a messenger brought the news that with ten thousand soldiers, Rana had launched massive attacks on the villages in Nimbahera, Javad and the adjoining areas, and Ambaji Pant, whom Devi Ahilya had sent to counter the enemies, had been killed in a battle near Chakharda. Hearing the news, Devi said, "Look Nana, how your cowardice has increased the enthusiasm of Chandravats. Had you countered them from the beginning they would not have dared to come so far."

Devi said, "It is not the first revolt of Chandravats. After the death of late Subedar Malhar Rao, when Tukoji Rao was in the South, they had risen up in revolt in 1771 taking full advantage of the occasion. But then, accompanied by Sharief Bhai, I had myself countered them. We had a fierce battle near a village Palsuda on the north of Mandsaur. With a sword in hand, I had myself taken part in the battle. After much bloodshed, Chandravats were defeated. Defeat of the enemy depends upon how much we are prepared for a bloodshed only to win the war. In 1783 also, when they had revolted, we made every arrangement to deal with them. Rajputs are taking my magnanimity as my weakness, hence this time I will have to decide over their fate forever."

Ultimately, with an object of crushing the frequent revolts of Chandravats forever, Devi Ahilya decided to send a huge army led by Sharief Bhai. She said to Sharief Bhai, "You will lead this mission. Our huge army will follow you. Go at once and crush the Rajput revolts forever. Fight a fierce battle, dig out entire Mewar region so that Rajputs do not dare to rise up in revolt against us. Remember one thing; if anybody fled from the battlefield, I will get him decapitated."

"Listen carefully. I want the heads of the rebels; I want a

dug up Mewar, I want the news that Rana of Chandravats has been blown alive in front of a gun. I want nothing less than this. If you feel unable to do this, I will myself come with a lance in my hands and destroy the enemies. But before that, I will punish the fugitives and truants of my own army." Thus at the urge of Devi, and led by Sharief Bhai, her army launched a massive attack on Rajputs. Devi herself reached in the battlefield and began to direct the soldiers from behind. She also carried out fresh recruitments to reinforce the dead and injured forces. She also supervised the treatment of injured; and also rewarded the soldiers who showed extraordinary courage.

Thus skilled leadership of Devi Ahilya and encouragement led to generation of exceptional enthusiasm in Holkar army. Like the agents of death, Maratha forces launched a massive attack on Rajput army. A fierce battle followed. Thousands of people died on both sides. Forces of Devi Ahilya uprooted the feet of Rajput army. In no time, Rajput forces began to run amok, victorious forces of Holkars reached Rampura and recaptured it.

Leader of the rebel Chandravats fled and took refuge in the fort of Amad. Devi's forces surrounded the fort. Devi's forces had a very famous gun 'Jwala'. Cannons fired by Jwala were showering destruction on the fort. At last, Devi's forces vanquished the fort and captured Saubhag Singh Chandravat, the leader of the rebels. By the order of Devi Ahilya, he was tied to the barrel of the gun and blown up. All the rebels surrendered and put down their arms. Thus, with firm determination Devi Ahilya crushed the rebellion.

When the news of Devi Ahilya's victory reached Poona, Shrimant Peshwa celebrated a victory festival. Guns were fired in the honour of Devi. Famous political, diplomat and savant courtier of Peshwa, Nana Fadnavis said, "So far, we have heard

about the praises of Devi Ahilya's piety. But we did not know that she is an amazon, who can rout her enemies. But today, we come to know that Maheshwar is a gateway of Poona on the bank of Narmada."

Nana Fadnavis was the 'think tank' of Shrimant Peshwa. He had the greatest influence on the contemporary history. Such a great personality was an admirer of Devi Ahilya and respected her. Chandravats had risen three times in revolt. First time in 1771, second time in 1783 and third time in 1787. On all the three occasions Devi Ahilya herself crushed the revolt. In 1771 she herself took part in the battle. In 1783 she sent an army to deal with the rebels, while in 1787, despite her old age she led her forces directly in the battlefield and sternly crushed the revolt forever. On all the three occasions, her commander-in-chief was away in the far South. Hence, Devi Ahilya had to fight these battle on her own strength. But working with super strategic understanding and cleverness she defeated seemingly indomitable enemies like Rajputs. All these victories led to an ever increasing popularity of her ability, diplomacy and gallantry throughout the country.

11
Unparallel Construction

It was a speciality of Holkar family that they did not use public funds to meet their personal and family expenses. For their personal expenses, they had a personal fund. Founder of the Holkar Kingdom, Malhar Rao Holkar had received, requesting Shrimant Peshwa, some properties in the name of his wife Gautamabai to meet the personal expenses of his family. Queen consort had the right to look after this personal property. Apart from the revenue generated from this property, property and precious items received by the Queen as gift also used to be deposited in the personal fund.

After the demise of Gautamabai, Devi Ahilya inherited the personal fund, which at that time contained about sixteen crore rupees. After the death of her only son Maley Rao, Devi Ahilya decided to use the property of personal fund in charitable works.

During the time of late Malhar Rao, Devi Ahilya had got ample opportunities to tour the various places of pilgrimage. She was thus fully aware that the expenses that are incurred for carrying out pilgrimage tours, outstation stay and feeding etc., were beyond the reach of the poor pilgrims. Those days, most of the places of pilgrimage lacked the proper

facilities for staying and dining at cheaper rates. Moreover, most parts of the country were under the rule of the Muslims. Hence, most of the temples and *Ghats* in the places of Hindus' pilgrimage were in miserable conditions. Devi Ahilya decided to spend the property of her personal fund in the renovation of these structures.

Apart from the construction of *Ghats* on the rivers throughout India, renovations and restoration of the temples that had been demolished by the foreign invaders, construction of hospices, digging of wells, stepwells and sumps and construction of the new temples, Devi Ahilya planned to start free public kitchens to feed poors and the pilgrims.

For the realization of her plan, she began lengthy discussions with the sages and saints and the pilgrims, who had visited various places of pilgrimage, to comprehend the problems and necessities of these places. According to the outcome of these discussions, she then drew a comprehensive plan to carry out the construction works. She wrote letters to all the kings of the country and requested them to send their skilled sculptors and artisans and appointed them for the construction works. Structures built by Devi Ahilya are visible in the uncountable places of pilgrimage across the length and breadth of India including Himalayas. From Badrinath and Kedarnath in the North to Rameshwaram in extreme South, and from Jagannathpuri in the East to Dwarka, Somnath in the West there is not even a single place of pilgrimage, which does not have a piece of sculpture and architecture built by Devi Ahilya.

Devi Ahilya did not consider end of her duty simply upto the construction of temples and other structures. For the maintenance of the structures built by her, she had arranged for a separate fund also. Devi understood well that all the buildings that she had got built, would soon turn into ruins if she did not arrange for their maintenance. She had seen dilapidated condition of the structures built by preceding rulers. Hence, Devi appointed many able and skilled professionals for the maintenance of the structures built by her and conducting the services she initiated and made permanent arrangement to fulfil their financial requirements. That is why, even two hundred years after the death of Devi Ahilya, structures built by her and the services that she initiated are still visible at every place of pilgrimage.

Structures built by her are technically excellent. They are exquisite examples of artistic work. All of them are excellent examples of Indian architecture. For the construction of the temples, Devi Ahilya had purchased the lands and transferred them to temple trusts. She had also appointed the priests, psalmists, preachers and religious savants and managers for the temples and had fixed their salaries from the state funds. She also made an arrangement of annual grant for the maintenance of these temples.

Devi Ahilya was a fervent devotee of Lord Shiva. Hence, she got maximum number of Shiva temples built. But she did not ignore other sects either. She got many temples of other deities built and restored. Evidences are also available that support the fact that Devi had issued grants for the religious places of other religions also like mosques and *Dargah* (shrines) etc.

Mughal Emperor Aurangzeb had demolished the famous Kashi Vishwanath temple in 1667. Devi Ahilya got this temple rebuilt in 1785. She got a 51 feet high temple as well as Jagmohan and Chakrapani temples built in Varanasi. She also got the restoration of old *Ghats* done and new jetties and sumps built. She also got a road constructed from Calcutta to Kashi. Famous Somnath temple, which had been demolished by Mahmud of Ghazni, was restored to new imposing structure

by Devi Ahilya.

Ancient Saptapuri, twelve *Jyotirlings* and *Chardhams* (four most sacred places of pilgrimage, each located in every corner of India—Badrinath in North, Jagannathpuri in East, Rameshwaram in South and Dwarka in West) are considered as the major places of pilgrimage in Hinduism. In all these places, Devi made proper arrangements for bathing, worshipping, prayers, staying and dining of the pilgrims. She established an ideal example of dedicated service. In the regime of Devi Ahilya, sculptures and artisans remained engaged continuously for thirty years in different parts of the country. Devi used to say, "This Holkari chisel must work continuously. Construction work must never be stopped." And indeed chisels and hammers of Devi continued to work relentlessly, examples of which are present throughout the country in the exquisite pieces of work.

One can imagine the inaccessibility of Badrinath, Kedarnath, Gangotri etc., two hundred and fifty years ago. These places of pilgrimage are more or less inaccessible even today. But Devi had no word like impossible in her lexicon, nor did she allow anybody to make excuses. In his book *Memories of Central India*, Sir Malcom writes that his associate, Capt D.T. Stuart managed to reach Kedarnath in 1818, facing many hurdles in the way. But he was amazed to see that even in that inaccessible remote place hospice and sump were present, which were built by Devi Ahilya. He also saw the public kitchen that served twenty-four hours a day run by Devi Ahilya in Giri Tirth of Dev Prayag.

Devi Ahilya had built her capital in Maheshwar. There she had got a huge jetty built on Narmada. Perhaps no other river in the world has such a huge jetty. For her own residence, Devi built a house at such a place from where she could easily see the religious activities taking place on the jetties of

Narmada. From the grove of basils in the courtyard of her residence, entire sacred ambience of Narmada bank was visible. Sir Malcom describes the Siddhanath temple which was built by Devi Ahilya, 'as the excellent temple architecture in Central India.'

At the same spot in Alampur, where her father-in-law, late Malhar Rao Holkar had breathed his last, Devi got a huge canopy-cum-cenotaph and a Harihareshwar temple built. Both these structures are exquisite pieces of architecture. At the place of her birth Chauri also, Devi Ahilya got a temple and a jetty built on the river. Two hundred and fifty years ago, means of transport were very limited in the country. Travelling from one place to another would require too much time. Besides there were every kind of dangers lurking on the way. Transportation of building materials was even more troublesome. But despite all those difficulties, construction works carried out by Devi Ahilya throughout the country still appear unparallel and amazing.

Devi Ahilya used to appoint the workers and the artisans for the construction works only after proper scrutiny. She also kept close watch on their work and account. Squandering, carelessness and corruption were unbearable to her. She took no time in removing such people from work.

During a construction work in Nasik, when she came to know about unnecessary delay and forgery in funds by a man, she at once removed that man from work. Similarly, she was suspicious about the strength of Shri Ram temple in Pantharpur. She, therefore, herself got the strength of the temple tested by making an elephant walk on its roof in her presence. Only after getting fully satisfied, she made the payment for the construction.

Every year on the *Ekadashi* (eleventh day) of *Asadh* and *Kartik* months, thousands of people used to visit Pantharpur

walking on feet. They used to have a sight of Lord Vitthal in Pantharpur. For their convenience, Devi Ahilya bought the agriculture rights in the surrounding forests, and got many stepwells and sumps dug on these lands and leased out the fields to the farmers for tilling on hereditary basis. She also made these farmers responsible for freely feeding the pilgrims with *Jhunaka Bhakar* (gram flour breads) and drinking water. At many other places in the country, Devi provided the people with land and cattles and made them responsible for offering free milk to the pilgrims. Descendants of these families remember these things with proud and express their gratitude to Devi Ahilya.

On the way to Omkareshwar and many other places of pilgrimage, Devi Ahilya had built many beautiful and artistic stepwells; many of which are quenching the thirst of the pilgrims even today. Bridge on Karmrashini river in West Bengal had also been built by Devi Ahilya. By her construction works she played an important role in arising a sense of devotion among the people for these places of pilgrimage.

12
Inspiration to Anant Fandi

During the regime of Devi Ahilya, there was a famous poet in Maharashtra. His name was Anant Fandi Gholup. A resident of Sangamner town in Maharashtra, this Brahmin was an ever wandering poet and a melodious singer. His voice was exceptionally sweet. Moreover, his singing style was equally impressive that turned the people mad after him. Whenever, taking a tambourine, he stood to sing, he left the listeners spellbound. Besides, he also used to sing in *Tamasha* (traditional folk theatre of Maharashtra). His singing had a far and wide reputation.

Once, having heard about the reputation of Devi Ahilya, this wandering poet started towards Maheshwar alongwith his troupe to see her. *En route*, when they were passing through the ranges of Satpura mountains, a gang of tribal Bheels looted them and brought the members of the troupe to their head. In the presence of the head, Anant Fandi began to sing on the beats of his tambourine which left all the Bheels and their head spellbound. When the head enquired, he told him that they were going to see Devi Ahilya and present their art before her in Maheshwar.

Mention of Devi's name made the head feel ashamed of

his deed. In a sad tone, he said, "We did not know that you are a great poet and going to present your art before Devi Ahilya in Maheshwar. Our men looted you by mistake. Had you told about yourself earlier, we would not have committed this sin. We now return all your belongings to you. Kindly do not tell Devi anything about the event." Then, the head of the Bheels sent four or five Bheels with Anant Fandi for his safe escort to Maheshwar.

After reaching Maheshwar, Anant Fandi appeared in the court of Devi Ahilya. He had donned a big turban on the head and inserted a crest into it. He had a big moustache and big ear-tops. He laid prostrate before Devi Ahilya. Other members of his troupe also bowed their heads. Then all of them stood showing great respect to Devi. All of them were spellbound by the sight of Devi and felt there lives blessed.

In reply to their greetings, Devi said, "Poet, you and other members of your troupe are popular in Maharashtra. Your reputation has reached us also. We are pleased to see you here. Now stay in our city for some days, and make our citizens familiar with your art." Anant Fandi said, "We have come so far from Maharashtra only to have a sight of *Matushri* and present our art before you and receive your blessings." Devi said, "My blessings and the grace of almighty God shall always be with you."

Anant Fandi said, "As per your dictate, we shall stay here for some time and exhibit our art. It is only by your grace that we stand alive before you. Had we not had your grace, our life would have ended in the way." Devi insisted them to relate all events that happened on the way in detail. Anant Fandi related all the events that had taken place on the way in detail and told how the Bheels looted them and tried to kill them. But when they sang the life sketch of Devi Ahilya on the tambourine, the head of the Bheels not only spared their lives but arranged for their safe passage upto Maheshwar also and begged pardon again and again for their abhorrent deed.

Devi instructed her officials to investigate the matter that why, in violation of her instructions, had Bheels started looting and plundering again. "When we have made every arrangement for their employment, why do they indulge in illegal job of looting and killing people. Warn them that if we again get any complaint against them, we will be forced to punish them."

Anant Fandi requested again, "*Matushri*, your grace has saved our lives. Hence, we desire to pass our lives in future as per your dictates. We also wish to present our art before *Matushri.*" Devi accepted their request. Next day, in the presence of Devi, they started exhibiting their art before the citizens of Maheshwar. In extremely melodious and happy voice, Anant Fandi began to sing. *Geet* (songs) *Lavani, Tamasha*; he presented every form of folk art and won the hearts of his audience. Pleased by his art, Devi presented him with valuable gifts. Anant Fandi was very happy to receive those rewards.

After presenting him the rewards, Devi said, "Fandi, you are a Brahmin and an excellent artist. Gracious God has bestowed you with a melodious voice and an art to write and sing the songs. You are using your art for entertaining the people. But you must rise above and think in different way. It is not proper for you to sing love songs only. Your art deserves even better utilization."

"You wander throughout the country, hence you are aware of the condition that prevails in the country. Hence, instead of singing love songs only, and entertaining the public, you must utilize your art for generating awareness among the masses. If you write good psalms in devotion of God and make efforts to generate devotion and love for the country among the people, I think you will do more justice with your art.

Hence, you must apply your art as a psalmist in the work of public awareness, instead of light plays, *Tamasha* and love songs."

"Instead of taking tambourine, take *Iktara*, forks and cymbal and sing the verses of Gyaneshwar and Tukaram, inspire the society to tread the path of virtue. I think only then you will use your art better. Should you take this work in your hands, I assure you that the responsibility of feeding your family will be mine. I will be happy if you could do so."

Anant Fandi bowed his head before Devi Ahilya and said, "*Matushri*, since long we have been performing our art throughout the country. We have been awarded in many royal courts for our art. But, we never saw a connoisseur of art like you. You have opened our eyes. As per your order *Matushri*, right from today, I will pass my life as a psalmist publicising devotion to God and the country and generating awareness among the masses."

Saying this, Anant Fandi lacerated his tambourine with a knife. Since then, he passed his life as a Psalmist spreading the message of devotion to God and taking to the virtuous course. Thus, the inspiration of Devi Ahilya changed the course of life of a wandering artist like Anant Fandi.

13

Death of the Grandson Nathyaba

Devi Ahilyabai's daughter Muktabai had given birth to a son in 1767. He was named Nathyaba. Devi Ahilya was very pleased by the birth of her grandson. Since her son Maley Rao had died issueless, Devi had no legitimate successor to her kingdom. In such a condition it was natural for her to be happy when her daughter gave birth to a son. It is also said that interest is dearer to a man than the real amount. Hence, he likes his grandsons and granddaughters more than he likes his own sons or daughters. Moreover, Nathyaba was the only son in the clan of Devi Ahilya; hence he became dearer to Devi. Most of the time, Devi kept him in her vicinity. She fostered him with great love and care and tried to culture him with good customs. She had a desire to make him the successor of the kingdom.

Nathyaba was very weak since his birth, and used to fall ill frequently. Devi made every attempt to improve his health, but he did not respond and his health could not be improved. At the age of twenty-one, Nathyaba acquired tuberculosis. For two years continuously, he suffered from fever and cough. His body was reduced to mere skeleton. Many *Vaidyas* and *Hakeems* treated him by all means, but in vain. His health could not improve. Those days, tuberculosis was an incurable disease.

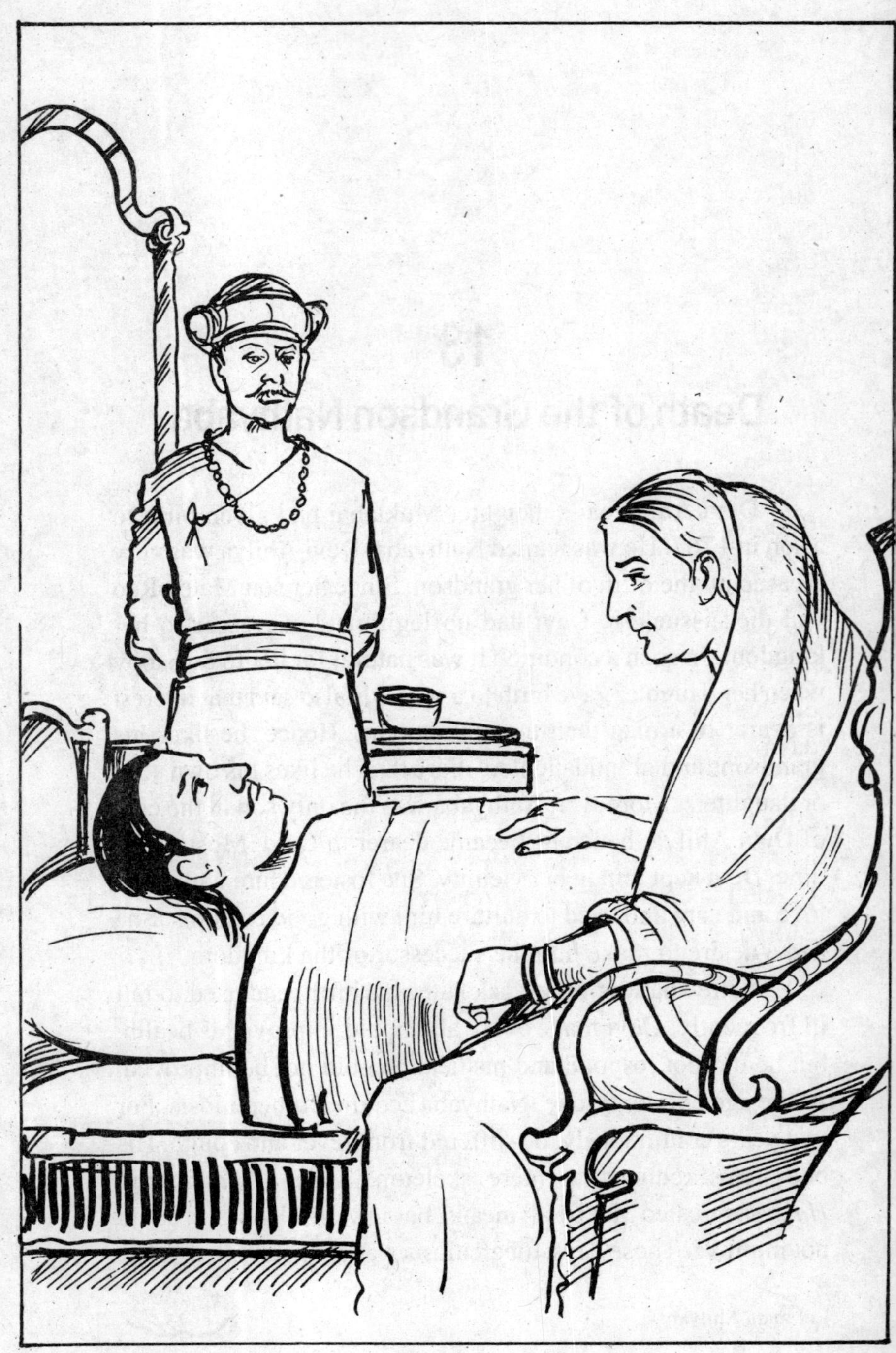

No *Vaidya* or *Hakeem* had an effective treatment for this deadly disease. Even Shrimant Madhav Rao Peshwa had died because of tuberculosis. Only the name of tuberculosis was enough to unnerve a person. As far as possible Devi Ahilya tried to get Nathyaba treated, but without any gain. The disease continued to grow. When treatments of charmers, *Vaidyas, Hakeems* etc., failed, Devi resorted to charity, making donations etc., with a hope that perhaps with the blessings of the poors, saints sages, and Brahmins etc., Nathyaba might be cured. After the death of her son, all of Devi's hopes came to centre at her only grandson Nathyaba. She left no stone unturned in the treatment of Nathyaba with a hope that one day he would bear the responsibility of the kingdom.

Devi Ahilya observed fasts; recited Lord's name and even pledged to make suitable offerings to please the God. Devi Ahilya did everything for the health of her grandson. She even donated gold equal to the weight of Nathyaba. But all of her efforts proved futile. Nathyaba's condition was deteriorating day by day.

Even the citizens of Maheshwar joined Devi in her efforts. Recitations and *Kirtans* continued in the temples. Recitation of even *Mahamrityunjaya* hymn was carried out. But nothing worked. On November 15, 1790, grandson of Devi Ahilya, Nathyaba closed his eyes for ever at a tender age of twenty-three.

He was survived by his old grandmother Devi Ahilya, his parents Muktabai and Yashwant Rao Fanase and two wives aged seventeen and ten respectively. Both these wives committed *Sati* with him.

14

Fate of Muktabai

Untimely death of their only son proved a severe blow for the son-in-law and daughter of Devi Ahilyabai. Their condition became critical. Mental condition of Yashwant Rao Fanase deteriorated to such a stage that he saw no pleasure in anything. Day and night grief engulfed him. Ultimately, his health too began to fall because of grief. All treatment failed to improve his health. Within one year after the death of Nathyaba, Yashwant Rao Fanase too died suddenly on November 3, 1791 because of cholera. Devi's only daughter had been widowed. Entire Maheshwar came to be shrouded by deep sorrow. Grief of Devi Ahilya had no limit. She was unable to contain her tears. At an age of sixty-six, even the last support of her life had fallen. All of a sudden, Devi's daughter told her about her decision to commit *Sati* with him. This decision completely broke Devi Ahilya. Now, only Muktabai had survived as her last support. After her committing *Sati*, the whole lineage of Devi Ahilya was about to end. All the attachments had ended that day. After her mother and father, in-laws, husband, son, brother, daughters-in-law, grandson, granddaughters-in-law and now her son-in-law and daughter were also leaving her.

Devi Ahilya tried hard to convince her daughter that considering her old age, she must give up her decision to commit *Sati*. But all her insistence failed. Muktabai stayed firm at her resolution. She said, "Mother, we two are the only survivors of our family. You will have no support after me, and I will have no support after you. At the time of our father's death, you had resolved to commit *Sati*. But at our grandfather's request and in order to look after the kingdom after him, you had changed your mind. You had a purpose to live your life. But I have no purpose in life. As far as your looking after is concerned, there are many people to look after you. Besides, much of life has passed. But if I don't commit *Sati* today, it would be extremely difficult for me to pass a purposeless life. Hence, it is better for me to commit *Sati* on the pyre of my husband."

Devi Ahilya had no reply to the logic of Muktabai, who was firm at her resolution. On one hand, hearse of Yashwant Rao was being decorated and on the other Muktabai was being adorned as a *Sati*. Scene of Yashwant Rao's funeral procession was really very tragic. His relatives, officials and thousands of citizens were walking mournfully in the procession. Muktabai and two other wives of Yashwant Rao were walking behind the bier. Muktabai's face was glowing with an extraordinary sheen. With folded hands, she was walking slowly behind the bier. Behind her and supported by many maidservants, was Devi Ahilya walking slowly. On the rear side of the procession, was huge crowd shouting *Jai...........Sati Mata*.

A huge pyre of sandalwoods was made on the bank of Narmada for Yashwant Rao Fanase. His body was placed on the pyre. Muktabai too sat on the pyre taking the head of her husband in her lap. Muktabai's face was glowing with divine brilliance. Amidst the recitation of Vedic hymns and loud sounds of musical instruments, the pyre was set on fire. The whole ambience was reverberating with the sounds of conchs, horns, drums and slogans of *Jai.... Sati Mata.* Very soon, huge flames engulfed the pyre and Muktabai with that. *Matushri* Devi Ahilya could not see the scene. She fainted and fell on earth.

15
Moments of Solitude

Matushri Ahilya had boundless grief after her daughter Muktabai became *Sati*. She could see nothing but sorrow around her. She had confined herself within the high walls of her palace. One by one, her grandson Nathyaba, her son-in-law Yashwant Rao and daughter Muktabai had left this ephemeral world. Now there was no one even from the side of her daughter in her clan. She was in a state of agony after this tragedy. All the mundane relations and bonds had broken and ceased to exist one by one. It was merciless irony of destiny that had inflicted cruel blows one after another on the religious minded and pious Devi, who illuminated the lives of millions of the people burning her own life like a lamp; who paved the way of not only physical but of the metaphysical pleasures for her subjects; who stayed away from worldly comforts and preferred to live like an ascetic, discharging her duties and who lived every moment of her life in a pious way remembering the name of God. The cruel destiny snatched every member of her family one by one and left her in a fathomless state of misery. Nobody else could have faced so much sorrow. But it was Devi Ahilya, who continued to tread the path of her duties like a person immune to the circumstances. Like *Dharamraj* Yudhishthir, who continued to walk ahead without looking back even when all his brothers and near and dear ones fell dead one by one, Devi Ahilya too continued to tread the path of duty in her life in an immutable manner.

But the final blow of destiny shook Devi Ahilya deeply. All her life began to appear quite worthless. Her own mind had begun to question the meaning of her life. She was unable to understand that she had lived an ideal life without committing the slightest sin, why then she had to receive the harsh punishment from destiny. Moreover, what is the significance of such a life that has to undergo all kinds of bitter experiences towards its final stage, while all through the life, a person had behaved religiously, always balancing her action on the scale of religion and irreligion. Why to live such a life? These thoughts constantly stirred the mind of Devi Ahilya. Worthlessness of the life sapped all the desires in her mind to live. Because of these indecisive reflections in her mind, Devi Ahilya cut off and confined herself within the precincts of her palace.

During these moments of lassitude *Matushri* Devi Ahilya recollected her whole life and analysed her conduct mentally. From her long life, she could not recollect even a single situation when she might have behaved in an irreligious way. She was unable to understand for which sin has God punished her so hard. Suddenly a thought struck her mind if she had committed a sin by not becoming *Sati* after the death of her husband. Was her decision not to become *Sati* at the urge of her father-in-law to look after the kingdom and the subjects, not like a blow of arrow on her own skin? But then a second thought overtook her that she was not the first woman who did not become *Sati* after her husband's death. Uncountable women are there in history who did not become *Sati* with their

dead husband, just to complete their mundane duties. But the society never pointed any finger at the chastity of these women. She also remembered that the practice of *Sati* was an exception in the *Pauranic* and ancient society of India. It has never been in a traditional or conventional form. In *Mahabharata* also, after the death of king Pandu, only Madri had become *Sati*, while Kunti had survived to carry out the duties of fostering his sons and other mundane responsibilities. But her chastity was never considered any less than that of Madri. In ancient India, choice of *Sati* with the dead husband was dependent more upon the discretion of the woman than any convention or social pressure. Hence, if the circumstances warranted, not becoming *Sati* was not a sin for them. What is the sin that she is being punished for? A thought was stirring her mind again and again that before her eyes many women of her family became *Sati* on the pyre of their husbands, just because of this merciless convention. But for the social convention, she could not stop them despite her desire. Many of those women were innocent girls, whose married lives had not even started. Lotus of whose lives was sacrificed before blooming to this cruel convention because of the death of their husbands. Even during these moments of lassitude, faces of those girls were conjuring up in her mind again and again. A thought was constantly perplexing her that despite her fervent wish, she could not save the lives of those girls because this convention had greater public support in the name of religion.

Devi Ahilya was reflecting over the causes that gave birth to this cruel convention. Possibly, this practice would have started in medieval period, when the country was constantly invaded by the Muslim, foreign invaders, who invariably let out a series of mass plunder and atrocities every time they defeated an Indian ruler. This practice would have started as a safeguard measure to protect the chastity of the Indian women from foreign insult and atrocities. In Rajputana, womenfolk used to end their lives in *Johar* even before gallant Rajput warriors entered the battlefield donning ochre costumes. On one hand their action generated detachment in the minds of their husbands, while on the other, it saved their chastity in the absence of their husbands. Possibly, in the beginning, practice of *Sati* might have been a form of *Johar*, which converted later into a social convention. This convention, however, assumed such a formidable form that apart from Rajput woman and the womenfolk of the soldiers, womenfolk of the common public and merchant class began to be sent forcibly to become *Sati.* Vested economic interests of the close relatives also played an important role in this willy-nilly. When a woman committed *Sati*, her relatives naturally got a right on her property. Even if a woman somehow managed to escape *Sati*, her property used to be usurped by her relatives or she was kept deprived of her right on her property. If such a woman had no son, she could not adopt one without the permission of the administration. In all such situations, her property either used to be usurped by her relatives or attached to the state.

Devi Ahilya had a contention that in her kingdom and her regime no woman was ever forced against her will to become *Sati*. Moreover, after taking over the rule in her hand, Devi had accorded full protection to the rights of the widows. In an ordinance, she had given the women complete rights in the property of their husbands after the death of their husbands. She had also provided the issueless widow with a right to adopt a son without the state permission. Position of the woman had improved a lot in the society because of these steps taken by Devi Ahilya and the cases of becoming *Sati* had come down.

Thus retrospecting her life during the moments of lassitude, Devi Ahilya had one satisfaction that though she might have not been able to end the practice of *Sati* legally,

but she had definitely been able to empower the women socially and economically providing them their just rights and thus practically eradicating the practice of *Sati* successfully.

As soon as Devi Ahilya reached this conclusion, her lassitude subdued. A sense of enlightenment overtook her that, "Pleasures and plight are in the hands of destiny. Gracious God has released me from the bonds of all attachments. My whole life is now for my subjects fully. Forgetting my sorrow, I have to work to remove the miseries of my subjects. This is the sole objective of my life now. Not much life is left for me; but I have much to do? She then decided to pay attention to the administration of state."

16
The Final Journey

After the death of Yashwant Rao Fanase, ignoring her insistence Ahilyabai's daughter Muktabai had become *Sati*. After Muktabai's death Devi Ahilya could see no purpose in life. Remembrance of her near and dear ones, who had left her one by one, was making her extremely sorry. Her subjects tried to console her in many ways and by all means pacify her mind, but all in vain. Devi's diet diminished day by day, and her body grew weaker. But the strong feeling to work for the welfare of people and dutifulness towards the kingdom had kept her active. She had kept herself active till her last breath to keep her pledge that she had once made to work for the welfare of the subjects, and the promise that she had made to her father-in-law to manage the state after him. But at the same time, she had been anticipating the possible plight of the state after her. Mere imagination of that plight was enough to aggravate her sorrow.

After the death of her son Maley Rao, and rejecting the advice of Diwan Gangadhar Chandrachur to adopt a son, Devi Ahilya had taken over the management of the kingdom into her hands. Later on, requesting Shrimant Peshwa she had got the rights of Malwa's Subedari transferred to commander-in-

chief Tukoji Rao. But there was a clear understanding between her and Tukoji Rao that as long as she lived, she would hold the management of the kingdom, while Tukoji Rao would lead the military expeditions. Tukoji Rao was a trusted associate of late Malhar Rao. He was, in fact, in their relation. He was very brave and strong, and had taken part in many battles with Malhar Rao. Tukoji Rao had great reverence for Ahilyabai and despite being older in age, he used to call her as *Matushri.* Devi too treated him as her own son. But Tukoji Rao was very raw in politics, besides being too credulous. Hence, misguided by his advisors, often he used to commit such blunders that brought severe reprimands from Devi. Many poker type people often tried to create differences between Tukoji Rao and Devi Ahilya, which occasionally led to bitterness in their relationship. Both the sons of Tukoji Rao—Kashi Rao and Malhar Rao were very unsuitable. They were fighting with each other for the power. In such a situation, Devi could not see a suitable person, who could run the kingdom well after her. Hence, worries and miseries of Devi Ahilya continued to grow. These worries for the kingdom and the miseries of the self led to even more deterioration in Devi's health. Unbearable sorrow and harsh commitment for the duties weakened her body even further. Now she had also grown old. How long would her body cope with her labour and miseries? At last, Devi fell ill. Now she had no charm for life. Hence some time she took and some time she did not take the medicines prescribed by the country doctors. All this led to heavy fluctuations in her health. No serious illness had afflicted her ever before. But old age is a disease in itself. Her body continued to grow weaker because of old age.

In 1795, in seventieth year of her age, Devi Ahilya had been discharging her duties and responsibilities with full faith, though she had continued to be ill. She had anticipated that

her end was near. It was the Hindi month of *Savan* (*Shrawan*). Devi had resolved to feed twelve thousand Brahmins. Constant worship and rituals were continuing in the temples. Her last time had approached. Physicians and country doctors were working hard. But Devi was fully prepared for her final journey. Summoning the Brahmins and poors, she donated them liberally. On August 13, 1795, corresponding to *Savan Badya Chaturdashi*, Devi had been taking only the Ganges water since morning. She summoned the Brahmins and donated them a cow for her salvation. Then reciting the name of Shambhu Mahadev, and with peaceful mind, like the *Yogis* Lok-mata Devi Ahilya merged with the divine light in her small hermitage-like residence on the bank of sacred Narmada in Maheshwar leaving lakhs of her subjects wailing behind her.

News of her departing for heavenly abode spread like wildfire. A huge crowd of people thronged in Maheshwar to have her last sight. Sorrow of the subjects knew no bound. With tears flowing from the eyes, all the subjects were making preparations for her final journey. Her cremation took place on the bank of Narmada in Maheshwar. At that spot now stands a huge canopy.

17
Rule of Devi Ahilya

Praja Sukhe Sukham ra Gyah
Prajanashch Hite Hitam!
Natmpriyam Sukham Ragyah
Prajanashch Sukhe Sukham!!

(Pleasure of the king lies in the pleasure of the subjects; and in the benefit of the subjects lies the benefit of the king. Anything dear to the king is not the pleasure of the king and his pleasure lies in the pleasure of the subjects only.)

This dictum of Acharya Kautilya's *Arthashastra*, formed the basis for the system of Devi Ahilya's rule. Devi used to say that the governance had come into being only for the benefit of the subjects. Governance and the governed must have the same relation as a mother has with her child. Devi Ahilya regarded her subjects as her own children and behaved with them accordingly. That was the reason why she had been treated as *Lokmata* in the hearts of her subjects instead of as a queen or a ruler.

Devi Ahilya used to say: "I have to discharge the responsibilities that the almighty God has rested upon me. My duty is to keep the subjects satisfied. I am responsible for everything that I do. I have to explain before God for my deeds."

Because of this belief Devi Ahilya used to test her every work on the criterion of public interest before actually doing it. Immediately after her enthronement, she first of all reinforced the internal peace and security of the kingdom. She even put her only daughter at stake to remove the terror of the thieves and bandits. She declared, "I will marry my only daughter Muktabai to such a person who removes the terror of the thieves and the bandits from the minds of my subjects." Her plan worked well and in a short span, peace reigned supreme in her kingdom.

Devi Ahilya then initiated reforms in the land revenue system of the kingdom. She divided the whole kingdom into three segments—Northern, Central and the Southern. Areas of Indore, Tarana and Rajputana were in the northern segment. Maheshwar and the adjoining areas were part of the central segment, while the areas to the southern part of Satpura were part of the southern segment. Northern segment constituted mainly of those regions from where *Chauth* was collected. Devi had simplified the system of recovering land revenue. She personally looked after the public fund and often carried out surprise inspection of the work of her officials. This always maintained a fear in the minds of the officials and so they did their job carefully. No official could dare to misuse his powers.

Devi knew well that for the progress of the country, growth of agriculture and commerce was essential. Hence, she paid special attention on the development of these two segments. She solved the problems of the farmers and improved their lot and provided them with all kinds of facilities. She made sincere efforts for the development of commerce as well. In her time also, many goods used to be imported into her kingdom from outside. Devi took full care that the interests of local producers and traders were not harmed. She offered the local producers and traders liberal incentives and facilities.

She promoted the commerce of indigenous cloth in the state by all means. She offered all help to the weavers to settle and set up their looms in Maheshwar because of which Maheshwar got a prominent place in the country. Maheshwari *Sarees* are still famous in the country.

She strengthened the security system of the kingdom. She got many forts built at different places and posted her army in those forts. She maintained a big army, and raised an army of the women also. But she did never use her army to expand the boundaries of her state invading other kingdoms. Instead, she used her army only for the security of the kingdom and to assist Shrimant Peshwa at the national level war expeditions.

She also paid special attention that no powerful or rich person could torment a powerless or poor person. She regarded it her foremost duty to protect the poor and the weak.

Once, in Indore, a trader named Devichand died issueless, survived by his widow. After his death, some state official issued an order to attach his property. Trader's widow reached Maheshwar and complained to Devi Ahilya about the matter. Devi's heart was filled with pity after seeing the plight of the widow. She reprimanded the concerned official and said that the widow had full right on the property of her deceased husband, and her property must be returned at once and such incidence should not recur in future.

Once, an issueless but rich widow from Nimar expressed her desire to dedicate her property to the service of the kingdom, because her relatives wanted to usurp the property. Devi said, "It is your property. You should yourself spend it in good works."

Working on advice of Devi Ahilya, that widow spent her

entire wealth in the welfare of the masses. Many people used to approach Devi with desire to dedicate their wealth to her service. Devi always advised such people to spend their wealth in the works of public welfare at their discretion. This behaviour of Devi inspired her subjects to carry out public welfare works.

A big population of the tribal Bheels was present in forests of the kingdom. These Bheels often used to rob the travellers who passed through the forests. Many local rulers and landlords had sheltered these Bheels and used their plunder as a means to increase their income. Their terror had made the travelling quite unsafe. Apart from the plunder, Bheels also used to recover a strange tax, *Bheel Cowrie*, from the passers-by. Devi summoned the head of the Bheels and convinced him; helped them in carrying out agriculture to feed themselves with honesty. But when the Bheels did not change their way, Devi launched a military action against them and crushed them with firm hand and punished the offenders. Many Bheels were thrown into prisons and many were hanged to death. This firm action was enough to bring the Bheels on right course. Begging pardon for their deeds, the Bheels accepted to obey her order. Devi provided them with arable lands and necessary agricultural implements, thus freeing her subjects from the terror of plunder by the Bheels.

Devi entrusted the Bheels with the responsibility of the security of the travellers who passed through their region. She also warned them that *Panchayat* of the concerned Bheel region would have to pay the compensation for any loot taking place in their region. Incidents of plunder and loot came to an end because of the strictness of Devi Ahilya.

Whenever Devi received complaint against anybody, she would allow the concerned person to present his clarification fully before taking any action against him, and always arranged to remove any complaint he himself might have. Once, she received information of some disturbances by the Bheels in areas adjoining Vindhyachal. Any other ruler would have sent an army to suppress the people causing disturbances. But Devi Ahilya first sent one of her ministers to learn about the problems of the local population. To the leader of the Bheels, Devi herself wrote a letter stating, "Disturbances take place only in that province where rights of the people are violated openly. Should a king, driven by sheer selfishness come to regard public funds as his private property and misuse it arbitrarily, subjects are bound to grow restless with such a king. I myself make efforts without any discrimination to safeguard the interests of the people. I am always ready to solve your problems. Why are you then causing all these disturbances."

"A king, who ignores the problems of his subjects; who wrecks havoc and injustice upon them; who saps his subjects and himself enjoys every pleasure; who sees the end of his duties in his vested interests, such a king has no right to rule, while every citizen has a right to raise his voice against him. But I understand that no such thing has ever occurred in my kingdom. I don't know, why are you causing disturbances, and what are you going to gain. Such a conduct is not at all proper with a ruler who is always ready to protect you and solve your problems. Come to me and tell me about your problems, I promise to help you with all my powers."

Devi's words had a transforming effect on the Bheels. Their problems were solved in a peaceful way. Devi had motherly sentiments for her subjects, hence she wrote personally to the Bheels, who were causing disturbances, and listened to their words sympathetically before carrying out any military action against them. Because of her gesture of goodwill forest-dwelling Bheels regarded Devi Ahilya as their mother and obeyed her dictates. No other ruler could have

controlled this tribe and tied them to his law and order with such an efficiency.

Devi Ahilya saw her own pleasure in the pleasure of her subjects and regarded their sorrow as her own sorrow. She always longed to see her subjects' prosperity in every way. She regarded the poverty of the people as the poverty of the kingdom and prosperity of the subjects as the pride of the kingdom. Such as a mother feels proud by the prosperity of her son, similarly Devi Ahilya felt pleased to see the prosperity of her subjects. She never eyed the wealth and prosperity of her subjects and thus never tried to snatch the wealth of the people.

Those days, people had no facilities like modern banks, and they had to keep all their wealth in homes in concealment. But at the same time, they had the fear of thieves and dacoits as well, hence they did not dare to exhibit or use their luxuries openly. Keeping horses and carts, travelling in palanquins, building big houses, engaging servants and attendants were possible for the people who enjoyed state privilege. But in the kingdom of Devi Ahilya, there was no fear from the thieves and the dacoits, hence people could use their wealth openly.

It is a duty of the king that he should treat all the subjects equally without any discrimination. This policy was fully followed in the kingdom of Devi Ahilya. She herself followed Hinduism; but the followers of the other religions had the same facilities as were available to the Hindus. Even the Muslims praised her religious tolerance freely. There is not even a single example of state interference in freedom of worship in the regime of Devi Ahilya.

Devi Ahilya knew well that the rights make a person arbitrary. Hence, she exercised hard control on the rights of her administrative officers. These officials were so strictly monitored that they always feared punishment from the state.

Hence, no official or government employee dared to work arbitrarily in an unrightful way. If complaints were received against any official of misbehaving with the public, she made no delay in punishing the official.

In that period, a system prevailed in most of the kingdom that whenever a rich man died issueless, and his widow wished to adopt a son, she had to pay a heavy tax to the state to receive permission. If she failed to do so, her property used to be attached. Devi Ahilya banned this system in her kingdom and granted every widow a right to adopt a child or appropriate herself the property of her dead husband.

She said, "Even the religious scriptures grant the wife of a man, who dies issueless, a right to adopt a child. State has no right to interfere with rights of a widow, granted by the scriptures. If the state imposes a tax in the name of granting permission, it is against the religion." Hence, she issued clear orders to accept applications for adopting a child and grant permission without charging any fees.

Her court always used to be open for her subjects. Anybody could approach her without hesitation and present his grievances before her. Devi used to listen to the complaint carefully and get it scrutinized impartially and do justice with the complainant. She used to punish the violator irrespective of his designation and status.

Malhar Rao, son of her commander-in-chief Tukoji Rao, had also become unruly. When Devi received the complaint against Malhar Rao's impertinence and plunder, she summoned him and tried to convince him lovingly. But when his behaviour did not change and he continued to torment the public, Devi got him arrested and put him in jail as a punishment.

Once, the chieftain of Mahidpur started collecting tax from the subjects unlawfully. Some people approached *Matushri* and lodged a complaint. Devi at once summoned the

chieftain and listened to the logics of both the sides. The chieftain was found guilty. He was ordered to return the money to the people and warned not to repeat that mistake in future. The chieftain had been reformed forever and the subjects praised the justice of *Matushri*.

Similarly, she got the complaint against the *Mamalatdar* of Chinchwad that he had been tormenting a person. Through a letter, Devi warned him that she would not tolerate such action again in future. She also instructed him to listen to the public carefully and satisfy them fully, and that any complaint against him in future would attract stern action.

A rich businessman named Khemdas had died issueless in Sirouz. His widow sought the permission to adopt a son but the officer concerned demanded a bribe of three lakh rupees. The widow paid the bribe at that time, but later on, at the advice of someone, she appeared in the court and told Devi Ahilyabai everything about the event. Indignant Devi summoned the officer at once and found him guilty after thorough investigation. She made the officer return those three lakh rupees to the widow, besides terminating him from the service and punishing him harshly.

Devi had the capability of identifying the right person. She had selected able and meritorious people and appointed them as per their ability. She was efficient in assigning right job to the suitable person and getting that job done in a suitable way. Officials appointed by her discharged their duties lifelong with superb efficiency and honesty. Devi too kept a continuous watch on their work and never failed to reprimand them if she found any carelessness or mistake in their work.

Devi Ahilya used to take full care of the comforts and conveniences of the state employees and their families. She had issued orders to distribute salaries to the employees on a fixed date every month. Salaries used to be fixed on the basis of the nature of work and the qualification of employee. Work of every employee was fixed. An employee used to be told about the nature of his work and his salary at the time of his appointment. Devi used to behave with the employee in a philanthropic and affectionate way. Once, she came to know that the daughter of an employee, who was posted faraway, was ill. She at once summoned for the information about the illness and arranged for her medical aid. She even wrote to the employee that should he required any help for improving the health of his daughter, he might write candidly at once.

Once, the *Kamavisdar* of Nagalwadi wrote in his letter to Devi Ahilya that he frequently had gripping pains in the abdomen. Devi at once arranged for his treatment. Another official informed in his letter about the illness of his mother and described the plight of the house due to that illness. Devi herself visited the home of that official and consoled him. Thus, the state employees used to tell Devi Ahilya about their personal problems in the official letters, and Devi took personal interest in solving their problems.

Employees too had great reverence and devotion for Devi Ahilya due to her intimate behaviour, hence, they used to be ready to obey her orders putting even their own lives at stake. Devi also used to honour the employees with rewards, who performed well. She even rewarded her loyal employees with huge immovable properties. Sustenance of the employees in their old age was the responsibility of the state. Devi Ahilya was fully aware of the rules and regulations prevalent in her kingdom. She therefore amended the faulty rules, formed new, public friendly rules and implemented them. She had a phenomenal memory, used to retain in her memory what she heard even once. Neither did she do anything against the law and harmful for the people nor allowed anybody to do such things. She ruled always keeping her prudence and the interest

of her subjects before her. Governing system of her kingdom in her regime came to the fore in the country as an ideal system only because of Devi Ahilya's unique governance and the efficiency and dutifulness of the meritorious and honest employees who worked under her able guidance. Peace, morality, piety and prosperity reigned supreme everywhere in her kingdom. Her governing system is considered as an ideal system, even today.

18
Justice of Devi Ahilya

Contemporary Marathi poet Moropant writes about Devi Ahilya—"O Devi Ahilyabai, you are blessed in all the three worlds. No other lady is as just and pious as you are in *Kalyug*. No one has ever seen or heard about any other lady as just and pious as you are."

Before the foundation of the Holkar Kingdom, number of the courts of law were just nominal in the Mughal rule. But after the establishment of the Holkar Kingdom, and during the regime of Devi Ahilya, courts of law were also set up in a systematic way. With an object of providing justice to the people, Devi appointed able judges. She even encouraged setting up of *Panchayats* at village level and gave them the right to do justice. During her regime *Panchayats* and the courts of law were playing an important role in providing justice to the people in a satisfying way. Detailed reports of the working of *Panchayats* and the courts used to be conveyed in a fixed time frame by the high officials of the state to Devi. On the basis of these reports and when required these rules and procedures used to be amended by Devi.

Any person, unsatisfied with the verdict of the court could appear in the court and present his complaint before Devi

Ahilya, who then herself used to give her ruling sitting on a high seat of justice. Her justice never failed to satisfy the involved parties. Her subjects had such a reverence for Devi that even the thought of rejecting or not accepting her verdict was assumed as a sin.

Justice was cheap and easily accessible in the *Panchayats* and the courts and used to be done without delay. It was not possible to influence the justice by wealth or muscle power. Justice was available to the poor and rich, powerful and powerless, common and influential people equally in an impartial way. In her personal life, Devi Ahilya was extremely merciful and forgiving, but when she occupied the seat of justice she would become totally impartial, just and strict towards her duties. She never showed mercy on the violator of propriety, rules, regulations and morality and those who harmed the interests of the public; nor she ever pardoned such people. A criminal always remained a criminal in her eyes; no matter whether he was an ordinary citizen or an official, chieftain, landlord or a member of the royal family.

Whenever a matter was brought to the knowledge of Devi that injustice had been done with a person because of administrative flaw, she at once used to issue order to correct the flaw and do justice with the concerned person.

Once a man named Ranoji Thite appeared in the court and presented some documents that showed that his grandfather, late Mahadji Thite Kenderkar had lent some money to late Subedar Malhar Rao Holkar for the purchase of two horses. The documents also showed that the loan was still due on the royal court. Devi at once scrutinized the documents herself and ordered the administration to pay back the years old loan.

Once twelve hundred rupees of a heirless man were deposited in the state exchequer by an administrative officer.

Later on, a brother of that man appeared in the court and proved his claim as the heir of that man. Devi immediately instructed the administration to return the money to the concerned heir.

On September 1, 1792, in a letter to Bharmal Dada, Devi Ahilya said, "You had wrongly accused Jakhoji Jagatap of Pargana Thalner Manju Baghadi and recovered four hundred rupees from him which you deposited in the state exchequer. Later investigation proved Jagatap innocent, hence return his four hundred rupees at once from the state exchequer."

These incidences are the self-explicit examples of Devi Ahilya's equitability. Any kind of injustice, whether it had been done by the state administration or the common man was unbearable to her. She neither did injustice herself, nor allowed anybody in her life to do injustice. Whenever Devi came to know about any injustice, she herself intervened to do away with it, no matter whether the wrongdoer was a high official of the state or an ordinary person.

Because of Devi Ahilya's equitability and their reverence and devotion for her, people often used to bring their family disputes before her for a solution. Devi too would candidly settle their disputes like the head of those families and the concerned parties would accept her decision contentedly. Many people would also present even the private matters of their families before her in a candid way and sought her advise and worked accordingly. Thus Devi Ahilya was like an affectionate *Matushri* not only for her subjects, but for the chieftains and landlords and even for the small kings and rulers.

Once a dispute set off between the contemporary Holkar and Gwalior kingdoms over a piece of land that was situated between them. The dispute continued for years without any solution. At last, both the parties decided to settle the dispute by the verdict of the *Panch*. Now the questions arose: Whom to appoint as the *Panch*? After prolonged deliberation, both the parties agreed on the name of Devi Ahilya as the *Panch*. Despite the knowledge that Devi Ahilya was herself the head of the Holkar Kingdom, Gwalior Kingdom had full faith in her ability and integrity, and hence did not object at all on her name. After listening to the logics of both the parties, Devi said in her unique verdict that both the parties should give up their claim on the land and leave it open as a pasture for the cows to graze in.

Both the parties accepted the verdict of the *Panch* with respect and left the land as a pasture without imposing any taxes on it. Even after independence, when both the kingdoms were merged in Indian union, that piece of land remained a pastoral land. This event shows how much faith did the people have in the justice of Devi Ahilya.

19

Economic Policy of Devi Ahilya

Money is required to run a kingdom. Huge amount of money is required for the security of the kingdom, to run the administration and for the development works. This money is recovered from the subjects as taxes. Manu Maharaj and Acharya Chanakya have defined an ideal king as per their hypothesis. Accordingly, a king who recovers minimum taxes and who frames a simple and clever taxation system, is an ideal king. In this view, Devi Ahilya can be regarded as an ideal ruler.

Devi Ahilya had an opinion that low taxes should be imposed on the subjects that they could pay easily. She believed that imposition of taxes more than the capability of the people would make the recovery hard on one hand and generate discontent and unrest in public on the other. Because of this belief of Devi Ahilya, her kingdom had lower taxes in comparison to the other kingdoms, whereas recovery of the revenue was higher.

After becoming the ruler, Devi Ahilya framed many new administrative and economic rules, while dismantled many old ones, which were not in favour of the subjects. She had clear opinion that the administrative rules must be framed in the public interest.

For the collection of taxes and land revenues, Devi Ahilya had divided her kingdom into districts and *Tehsils* and appointed able officials in those entities. She had given the village *Panchayats* wide authority. In her regime, *Panchayats* were very effective entities that worked well for the welfare of the public.

Devi had paid particular attention to the development of agriculture and the farmers. She had provided the farmers with every facility, and instructed the state officials to solve the problems of the farmers on priority basis. Efforts were made to improve the quality of agriculture and expand its limits. Devi showed no laxity in compensating for the losses in agriculture due to excessive or scanty rainfall and movement of the armies through the fields. In such situations, land revenues used to be waived off, besides providing other reliefs.

Tax on the agriculture was very low in the kingdom. Many kinds of other taxes were not applicable on the farmers. Besides, farmers did not have to fear the undue interference of the state officials. Farmers were therefore very happy. State had all kinds of edible materials in ample quantity due to bumper harvest. Grain markets had overflow of cereals. Cereals, milk, *ghee*, oil and many other essential commodities were available easily and at cheaper rates. Agriculture flourished in all round way during the regime of Devi Ahilya. Moreover, during the thirty-year long rule of Devi, Malwa did never suffer any famine, even for once.

She made sincere efforts to increase the trade in the kingdom as well. Since, peace prevailed everywhere in the kingdom, even the outside traders brought their goods fearlessly into the kingdom and traded freely. Kingdom had a flourishing business of the imported goods also. Cloth industry, developed by Devi Ahilya in Maheshwar was also flourishing

well, and the clothes and *sarees* produced in Maheshwar had good demand all over the country. Taxes levied on different goods were also fixed. Tax rates were comparatively low, hence they did not affect the trade unfavourably. Traders paid the taxes honestly, while corruption was virtually unknown among the state officials.

Devi Ahilya took special care in protecting the traders from the harassment of state employees. For this purpose, she had simplified and classified the rules. Devi had strictly instructed the officials not to collect even a single rupee more than the fixed tax. Whenever she came to know that any official had charged more than the fixed value, she made every arrangement to punish the official and get the extra money returned. Collection of the taxes and loans were done in a humane way. Stern measures were applied only when a person tried dishonestly to embezzle the loan despite his position to pay back.

Once, some of the state officials suggested that on some goods, the taxes were low in their kingdom, while the neighbouring kingdom had higher taxes on the same goods. Hence, those taxes should be increased to the corresponding level of the neighbouring state. Devi Ahilya stated in clear words that, "Evaluation of taxes is done keeping in mind our own circumstances and requirements and not on the basis of the taxes prevailing in the neighbouring kingdom. Hence, any increase in the taxes on the basis that they are higher in the neighbouring state, will be unjust." She also said that, "Taxes on the items that are essential for life, must be minimum, hence, we ought to reduce the taxes on these items, instead of increasing them." Thus, ultimately, she further lowered the taxes on those items in her kingdom.

During the rule of Devi Ahilya, taxes were so low that the public felt no pain in paying them. Hence, the people paid the taxes honestly. People also knew that the taxes paid by them would be spent for the welfare of the public. Because of this public belief, recovery of revenue was higher in Devi Ahilya's kingdom despite very low tax rates in comparison to the other kingdoms.

20

Defence Policy of Devi Ahilya

Except the three rebellions of Chandravats and the invasion by Rana of Udaipur for the help of Chandravats, all of which were controlled successfully by the efficient strategic leadership of Devi Ahilya, peace generally reigned supreme in her kingdom. Neither any feudatory raised in rebellion nor any other kingdom dared to attack Malwa Kingdom. Piety, equitability and goodwill of Devi Ahilya as well as her huge army and efficient war strategy were the main reasons for this condition.

Army of Devi Ahilya had fought many battles under the leadership of her commander-in-chief Tukoji Rao. But all those battles were fought on national level in association with Shrimant Peshwa. None of these battles had any direct influence on Devi's kingdom. Devi Ahilya however continued to supply Tukoji Rao with forces, ration and other warheads regularly besides providing him financial help from time to time. It was because of the help and the guidance provided by Devi Ahilya that Tukoji Rao always emerged victorious in those battles.

Once for the recovery of taxes from the king of Jaipur, Tukoji Rao was marching towards Rajputana along with a huge army. On the way, army of Sindhia launched an attack on Tukoji Rao's army. Tukoji Rao at once sent message to *Matushri* and requested her to send some forces and money. Devi was very angry by the attack of Sindhia. She at once sent five lakh rupees and a reinforcement of eighteen hundred strong force, and wrote, "Don't panic, defeat the enemy before return. I will form a bridge of money and army. If you still face any problem, write to me, I will myself arrive in the battlefield."

This inspirational message of Devi Ahilya worked wonder, and Tukoji Rao's army got a thumping victory in the battle.

Devi Ahilya had been renowned for her pious life, restoration of religious places and administrative efficiency. But she also paid special attention towards keeping her army alert and strong for the security of her kingdom. That was why, no enemy could ever dare to eye her kingdom with evil intention. And that was the reason why the peace reigned supreme in her kingdom and she could concentrate on the works of public welfare.

Devi Ahilya had furnished her army well with all kinds of weapons and trained the soldiers well in warfare. Godowns of ordinances and edible items were also kept ready with full supply. Devi herself took full care to see that her soldiers received their salaries and other facilities in time. She also took care of the families of the soldiers who were away in the battlefield. Responsibility of fostering the families of the soldiers, who laid their lives in the service of the country, rested upon the kingdom. Soldiers used to be satisfied by the affectionate behaviour of *Matushri* Devi Ahilya and fought the battle with all their strength and always returned victorious.

Army of Devi Ahilya had full faith in her. Once her commander-in-chief, Tukoji Rao tried to instigate his soldiers to fight against Devi, because he had developed some bitterness with her. But the soldiers plainly refused and said, "By your orders, we can fight against any enemy. We can even raise our arms against Shrimant Peshwa. But whether we live or not, we will never raise our arms against *Matushri*."

Devi Ahilya neither had a desire to expand her kingdom, nor any greed to plunder the wealth of other kingdoms. Still she maintained a huge army only to secure the boundaries of her kingdom. She did not even waste her wealth in raising unnecessarily huge army. Her army was small but highly skilled in warfare and disciplined. Her army was fully capable in maintaining internal peace as well as defending the external boundaries of the kingdom. Moreover, her army made remarkable contribution in strengthening Maratha empire taking part in national level war expeditions.

Devi Ahilya had been educated, trained and initiated by an excellent commander-in-chief, late Subedar Malhar Rao Holkar. Naturally, she had inherited many traits of Malhar Rao's personality. Consequently, she was as skilled as Malhar Rao in leading the forces and forming strategic arrays. Right from her teenage, she had taken part in many military expeditions with Malhar Rao. In the battles, she used to ride horses and led the forces like male soldiers taking arms in hands.

In the time of Malhar Rao, the kingdom had been divided into eighteen divisions and a *Saranjami* (chieftain) had been appointed in each of these eighteen divisions. Every chieftain had under him an area that generated one lakh rupees as revenue annually. So every chieftain had to keep an army in a certain strength and when the need arose, this army had to be sent in the battle. Devi maintained this system of chieftains in her regime also. Despite according them full honour, Devi Ahilya exercised full control on the chieftains. In 1772, on the direction of an American commander-in-chief Col Bride, Devi had raised an army in the Western style. The military pact with Col Bride is an excellent example of her far-sightedness and diplomacy.

Devi Ahilya worshipped peace. She did not like wars, hence she never started any war on her own. She even worked till last moment to work out a peaceful solution of the disputes and to avert the wars imposed by others. But whenever she entered the battlefield, she fought like *Ranachandi* and annihilated her enemies. During the revolt of Chandravats, she captured the leader of the rebels Saubhag Singh and got him blown up alive in front of the barrel of her famous gun 'Jwala'.

21
Religiosity of Devi Ahilya

Life of Devi Ahilya is an excellent example of religiosity. Since her childhood, she had been a fervent devotee of Lord Shiva. She had her first meeting with Malhar Rao at the Shiv temple in the village Chauri. Even after her marriage, when she became the daughter-in-law of Holkar family, her culture of religiosity accompanied her. She was even determined to become *Sati* after the death of her husband as per the prevailing convention. But she was forced to give up her resolution at the insistence of her father-in-law in favour of the subjects of the kingdom. After that incidence, worship of God and service of her subjects had become the sole objective of her life.

Service, renunciation, expiation, and making donation have always been a significant part of our *Sanatan* (eternal) culture. Accepting the existence of God in all the organisms and thus serving them with complete devotion has been assumed as the service to almighty God. The way with which Devi Ahilya served her subjects unselfishly, despite being the owner of a huge kingdom, has no parallel in history.

Devi Ahilya had dedicated her kingdom to Lord Shiva and ruled the kingdom as a representative of Lord Shiva. Her edicts used to be issued in the name of Lord Shiv Shankar.

She even dedicated the personal fund of sixteen crore rupees in the service of God putting basil leaves on it. With the money of the fund, she got restoration of the temples and places of pilgrimage done throughout the country.

Her whole life passed in making donations and serving the people. She did not confine her services within the limits of her kingdom. Entire country was her arena and the service of the entire humanity her object. She worked to remove the miseries of every human being with a feeling of *Vasudhaiva Kutumbakam*—i.e., the whole world is a family. Her affectionate and merciful motherly heart used to melt after seeing the agony of a person, and she would make every effort within her power to remove his or her misery. Her life is a unique example of platonic *Karmyog* (detached action).

All through her life, Devi Ahilya undertook innumerable construction works throughout the country. Constructions done by her and the services started by her in all the places of pilgrimage of the country continue even today.

Devi Ahilya could not see any person in misery and dire condition of starving and suffering. Hence, to remove the miseries of such people she regularly donated food, cereals, clothes, money etc. No beggar ever returned empty-handed from her doors. On festivals, she used to distribute new clothes and food among the poor. Apart from the capital Maheshwar, special arrangements used to be made in other towns as well for the help of the poor and the needy.

In the places of pilgrimage many food regions and public kitchens had been started where food and clothes used to be distributed among the poor, helpless people. Devi did not want to publicise about her services and win public applaud. She never listed her works of charity. Hence, no authentic information is available about the places where she started charity work. But from Badrinath in Himalayas, to

Rameshwaram in the extreme South and from Jagannathpuri in the East to Dwarka and Somnath in West, wherever we go, we find the constructions done and the services started by Devi Ahilya.

She honoured the Brahmins and savants of *Vedas*. She had conferred state honour on many such Brahmins and donated to them houses, land and even villages and granted them the right to hold these properties generation after generation. She appointed those Brahmins in the temples built by her for carrying out regular worships, rituals, preachings etc. In Maheshwar as well as in other places of pilgrimage, she organised regular worship, recitation, rituals, singing of devotional songs, narration of *Puranas* etc., engaging thousands of Brahmins and arranged for their food also. She had made arrangements for the sustenance of lives of many learned Brahmins.

During *Chaturmas*, religious fervour used to be worth watching in Maheshwar. In 1781, Pashwas' counsellor Vitthal Shamrao had written in his letter to Peshwa, "Here in Maheshwar, religious fervour is worth watching in the month of *Shrawan*. Daily about two to two and a half thousand Brahmins dine in public suppers. Three hundred Brahmins have been engaged in rituals, hundred in *Shiva Kavach*, one hundred fifty in *Shiva Smarana*, hundred in *Suryanamaskar* and hundreds of other Brahmins have been engaged in other religious activities. All these Brahmins are fed daily with delicious foods, given donations and other precious gift items." In another letter, Vitthal Shamrao told Peshwa, "On the occasion of the eclipse, Devi Ahilya, has donated cereals, gold and cash etc., worth rupees one lakh. She has also donated an elephant." In the month of *Shrawan*, thousands of Brahmins from northern India, Gujarat, Maharashtra and other provinces used to congregate in Maheshwar every year to take part in the religious rituals.

Devi Ahilya had made many secret donations also. At many places of pilgrimage, arrangement for the clothes of the idols of the temples, ornaments, oblation, lamps, worships and donations etc., had also been made permanently by Devi Ahilya. For the idols of God in Pantharpur, Rameshwaram and Kashi, she had donated ornaments of gold and gemstones. She had also made permanent arrangement for carrying the holy water of the sacred Ganges from Gangottari to the forty places of pilgrimage to conduct the ceremonial bath of *Shivalingas* on the occasion of *Maha Shivratri* every year. This tradition continues even today. Descendants of the Brahmins appointed by Devi Ahilya, still carry out this ceremony.

Sacred Ganges and her holy water have greatest significance in the religious sentiments of Hindus. Starting the permanent arrangement of carrying of the holy Ganges water from Gangottari to the places of pilgrimage situated in remote corners of the country for the ceremonial bath of the deity, Devi Ahilya had strengthened national unity. Apart from Hinduism, Devi had carried out construction work at the places of reverence for other religions also. At many places throughout the country, she had donated lands, estates, wealth etc., to the mosques, *Durgahs* (Moslem shrines), *Maulavis* and *Faqirs* etc., liberally. She had got restoration of many mosques done, and made regular donations to many mosques, *Durgahs* etc.

She not only had pity for the human beings, but she had equal pity for the birds and animals also. In many places, she had bought fields and left them open for picking by the birds. She had also made arrangements for sprinkling of wheat flour in the forests for the ants and flour balls daily in the rivers and ponds for the fish.

Devi Ahilya had great reverence for the cows also. She had made arrangements of the fodder and water for cows and

their calves at different places. In every village, pastoral lands used to be left for the grazing by the cattles. During summer, arrangements used to be made to avail drinking water at different places. In winter, blankets used to be distributed among the poors. Devi had appointed independent employees for the purpose. All these services used to be run from the personal fund of Devi Ahilya. To maintain this system on permanent basis she had made an independent permanent system without any support from the state exchequer. That is why, those systems started by Devi Ahilya continued in original form despite changes of rulers after her.

Tales of Devi Ahilya's munificence attracted many people towards her court. Those people would tell her the sad tale of their miseries and sought help from her. But Devi Ahilya would always investigate the suitability of those seekers. Once a Brahmin arrived from Kashi and told that his house had been gutted in fire and he had been rendered homeless. Thus, the Brahmin requested Devi to help him financially to build his house. Devi asked the Brahmin to stay in Maheshwar for some days and arranged for his stay and food etc. After about a month, Devi did not give him even a single rupee. So the Brahmin started back in dismay and reached Kashi in six months travelling via Rajasthan. But when he reached Kashi, he discovered that his house had been fully restored by the order of Devi Ahilya. In fact, holding the Brahmin in Maheshwar, Devi had instructed her men in Kashi to check if the Brahmin was telling right and arrange for the restoration if it had really been gutted in fire. This event shows that Devi never trusted the tale of anybody without checking its authenticity.

Because of liberal donations, public welfare works and charitable services, Devi Ahilya had become known throughout the country as *Lokmata*. From big kings and *Nawabs* to saints and sages and common people had great respect and reverence for Devi Ahilya. During her regime, no thief or dacoit ever dared to plunder the regions run by her. Even those cereal sheds that stood amidst dense forests remained safe from the thieves and dacoits, because plundering these cereal sheds was considered as sin by the outlawed. They feared that plundering of those cereal sheds would attract curse of pious Devi Ahilya Mata.

22

Interstate Relations in the Regime of Devi Ahilya

In the regime of Devi Ahilya, Holkar Kingdom was one of the prominent and powerful kingdom of the country. Naturally, Devi Ahilya was a respected and honourable figure in all the kingdoms. With the purpose of holding talks on the relations with other kingdoms, every kingdom used to appoint its representatives, who were known as *Vakeel* (counsellor) those days, in the capital of all the prominent kingdoms. Kingdoms like Poona, Gwalior, Bharatpur, Jaipur, Jodhpur and many other had their permanent counsellors in Maheshwar. Moreover, to discuss the prevailing national condition with Devi Ahilya counsellors of many other kingdoms also used to visit Maheshwar frequently.

Devi Ahilya too had appointed her counsellors permanently in Poona, Gwalior, Udaipur, Jaipur, Hyderabad, Ayodhya, Nagpur, Lucknow, Bhopal, Kota, Delhi, Srirangapatanam, Calcutta, Dungarpur, Pratapgarh and many more kingdoms. It shows that Devi Ahilya had developed interstate relations with the rulers of these kingdoms and maintained contacts with them to secure the issues of mutual interests. Through the counsellors, Devi would continuously receive the detailed report of the activities and political developments not only of that kingdom but of the other kingdoms in the region also. And through the same counsellors, Devi continuously held parleys with the rulers of those kingdoms.

Holkar Kingdom was a constituent of the greater Maratha empire, and hence was under the dominion of Shrimant Peshwa of Poona. During the regime of Devi Ahilya, constituents of Maratha empire had grown stronger with the result that Peshwa no longer had a control over them as he used to have before. But Devi accorded Peshwa full importance and honour thus maintained cordial relation with him. Thus working with superb diplomacy, she maintained the supremacy of Peshwa on one hand and on the other she managed to retain independent existence of Holkar Kingdom by his blessing. She had full regards for Peshwa and never did anything against his will. She used to cooperate fully with Peshwa in his planning and provided forces and money for his military expeditions. She had even instructed her commander-in-chief Tukoji Rao to obey Shrimant Peshwa first. In a letter to Peshwa his counsellor Hingane had written about Devi Ahilya, "Piety, intelligence and religiosity of Ahilyabai is going to make this institution permanent. She had full loyalty, trust, respect, dutifulness and enterprise for Peshwa."

Devi Ahilya accorded full honour to Peshwa and obeyed his orders as well, but she never welcomed any outside interference in the internal affairs of her kingdom. She held parleys with Shrimant Peshwa, Nana Fadnavis or her own officials on the matters of the kingdom, but only when it became necessary. Final decision, however, used to be of Devi Ahilya herself. Her opponents in the court of Peshwa used to hatch conspiracy against her, but she had so much influence

on Shrimant Peshwa that conspiracy of her opponents never succeeded.

Shrimant Peshwa too had great honour, respect and reverence for Devi. He always addressed her with great honour in his letters, and would often consult her in political matters.

Devi had cordial relations with her neighbouring kingdoms. Except the rebellions of Chandravats, not even a single occasion arose during her regime when she had to wage a war with any of her neighbourhood kingdoms. She never attacked her neighbouring kingdom with an ambition to expand her territory, and because of her strong army, none of her neighbouring kingdoms ever dared to attack Holkar Kingdom.

Peace, justice, equality and friendly coexistence with the neighbouring kingdoms were the main principles of her external policy. Rulers of the neighbouring kingdoms approached Devi Ahilya faithfully for guidance wherever some administrative or political disturbances arose in their states. Devi too readily obliged them with right guidance and advice.

In the contemporary India, she had cordial relations with almost all the kings, kinglets, Nawabs and Nizams. They too had great honour and reverence for Devi. Even the emperor of Delhi, Nizam of Bijapur and Tipu Sultan of Karnataka were very impressed by her.

Mahadji Sindhia of Gwalior was regarded as an influential force in the northern India. He was a powerful commander and a shrewd diplomat. But more than often, Devi Ahilya had outweighed him on the chequerboard of diplomacy. Despite his diplomatic defeats, Mahadji Sindhia had great respect and honour for Devi, and used to address her as *Matushri*.

British had begun to get foothold in India during the regime of Devi Ahilya. Because of her farsight Devi knew well that unless and until, those white foreigners were not driven away from the country, they would create big problem in future. In one of her letters, she had expressed this feeling in very clear words—"British have planned to expand in all the four directions. They are raising platoons at different places. In such situations, they should be crushed before their power grows any further, so that they fall in terror and do not try to advance again. Marathas, Nizams, Nawabs and all the forces must unite to crush the British."

This assessment of the increasing British powers by Devi Ahilya proves her farsightedness and superb diplomatic understanding.

23
Personality of Devi Ahilya

Devi Ahilya was born in an ordinary family. As per the contemporary conventions, she had been deprived of all those facilities that used to be available to the menfolk. But despite all adverse circumstances she achieved by her ideal life and unmatched deeds a supreme position that is unique in the history of the world.

Devi Ahilya was plain looking with somewhat darker complexion, well built, medium stature and having long black and dense hair. Her forehead was impressive, eyebrows long, bow-like and eyes huge and deep. Her visage reflected a pure and holy heart. She appeared like an incarnation of *Devi* (female deity). Hard work, disciplined life and simple vegetarian food had rendered her body active and efficient.

Her living style and costumes were simple and unostentatious. After the death of her husband she had stopped wearing ornaments and coloured clothes. She would wear plain, white *saree* only. Those days, veiling system and many other ostentations were prevalent among the women of royal families. But Devi was not to accept any tradition blindfoldedly. Keeping the womanly decorum, she maintained a distance from the veiling system. Often, it is seen that those people, who reach to the top despite their ordinary birth, acquire egoistic attitude. But it did not apply to Devi Ahilya. She was born in an ordinary family, and had become the head of a prosperous kingdom, but her nature had not changed at all. Ego too could not get a hold on her mind either. She was like a mango tree laden with fruits, the cool shade of which comforts human beings. She was like that basil plant, every leaf of which dedicates itself for the benefit of humanity. Her entire personality glowed with the brilliance of holiness, knowledge and spirituality. Her behaviour with her subjects was not like a ruler, but was more like an affectionate mother. She received everyone with an open heart regardless of the status of the comer. She was not partial or biased for anybody. She behaved with the common people, and her attendants in a cordial way. Even the attendants of her palace used to dine in the same dining room in which Devi would dine. She might have been a stern ruler for the evil and atrocious people, but for the common subjects, she was always an affectionate mother.

Devi had great contempt for injustice, sin and evil deeds, while she felt greatly satisfied to see the good deeds of her subjects. Failure by a person to discharge his duty and immoral and criminal acts performed deliberately always infuriated her. At that time, even the closer ones could not dare to approach her. Irreligion, atrocity, injustice and sinful conduct were unbearable for her. Craftiness or selfish conspiracies had no place in her life.

Devi Ahilya always respected the elders, but she never failed to reject firmly any undue pressure exerted even by an elder. She had great honour for Mahadji Sindhia of Gwalior. Mahadji too addressed her respectfully as *Matushri*. Once he visited Maheshwar for some official work. He stayed there for many days and received warm treatment. Then one day,

gathering his courage, he expressed his real political intention before Devi Ahilya. Devi did not agree to him, so she refused plainly. Indignant Mahadji said, "Keep in mind *Matushri*, that after all I am a man, and you might fall in trouble should we decide not to assist you. Also think about your situation if we decide to oppose you."

Anger of Devi saw no boundation after hearing the challenge of Mahadji. In a thundering voice, she said, "Mahadji Baba, such as you swallow the womenfolks of the household like a piece of betelnut, you can advise Tukoji the similar thing. But if you have courage, both of you may launch an attack on me with your armies. But remember one thing, that the day you come with your armies, I will welcome you chaining in the chains that is used to tie the elephants, otherwise, I will give up my designation of late Subedar Malhar Rao Holkar's daughter-in-law. You have given your feelings a vent, now come to act on your words, then I will also see you."

Even a brave warrior and diplomat like Mahadji forgot his leaps after hearing the bitter reprimands of Devi. Somehow, he soothed her anger with sweet talks and took leave hastily. In future, he never put on his courage again to show any craftiness with Devi.

Courts of the kings and kinglets are usually full of greedy toad eaters. But Devi Ahilya did not like such toady people at all, nor she offered them any shelter. Once a poet appeared in the court. He had brought his verses in which he had exaggerated exaltation of Devi Ahilya. Taking her permission, he began to recite his verses. His book contained poetic exaltation of Devi's virtues and greatness. For a while, Devi kept listening, then interrupting him she asked, "Does your book contain anything else, other than my exaltations?"

Poet said, "No *Matushri*, it contains your exaltations only."

Devi said, “It is enough. Keep the book here.”

The poet, kept the book on the floor. Calling her attendants, Devi asked them to immerse the book in Narmada, and said to the poet, “Had you utilized your talent in the exaltation of God, instead of creating verses in my praise, your life would have been more meaningful.”

Devi sent back the poet without any reward. Diligence and dutifulness of Devi Ahilya were really unearthly. She made continuous and relentless efforts to manage her kingdom and for the welfare of her subjects. She discharged her duty day and night daring all kinds of weather, fatigue and illness. She did not have any lethargy or leisureliness. She did not like laxity in work. Disciplined life and systematic working style were her main speciality.

It was unbearable for her that anybody would regard her weak because of her being a woman. She always dared the challenger with courage, and proved her excellence defeating him. All the famous royalties of that time had been defeated by Devi in the battlefield as well as in the arena of politics and diplomacy. All of them then had to accept her excellence. Even among the contemporary men, there was no one who could be compared to the multifarious personality of Devi Ahilya. Personality of Devi Ahilya was indeed lofty like the Himalayas and unparalleled.

24

Daily Chores of Devi Ahilya

Devi Ahilya was the ruler of a huge and prosperous kingdom. Had she wished all the pleasures and comforts would have been easily available to her. But Devi renounced all the comforts and made dutifulness and the service of the downtrodden sole object of her life. Her life is an ideal example of platonic and detached work. Like an ascetic, she renounced all the physical pleasures, and passed her life in the service of her subjects.

Everyday, she would get up one hour before the sunrise. Then she would go to the *Ghat* on the bank of Narmada and take her bath. Worship and self-study followed then. Then she would listen to the recitation of *Ramayana, Mahabharata, Vedas, Upanishads,* or *Puranas.* An authority on the religious scriptures, Pt. Ambadas Puranic used to read out scriptures for her and hold discussions with her on the scriptures. This sequence continued even whenever Devi fell ill. After listening to the scriptures Devi used to make donations. Cereals, clothes and money used to be donated to the Brahmins, beggars and helpless disabled people. All the guests used to be fed with respect. At that time Devi would see that nobody in the palace should remain hungry. When she made sure that everybody

had dined, only then she would sit down to dine. She always took plain vegetarian food. Though non-vegetarian food was common in the society and in her family, but she never ate non-vegetarian food in her life. She used to dine only once in a day. In the evening, she would take fruits instead of a full diet.

Her dining room and store room were very big. Able workers had been employed there. Apart from Devi, other members of the royal family, invited guests, Brahmins, who carried out rituals, knowledgeable *Pundits*, employees of the royal palace and attendants, in all about three to three hundred and fifty people used to dine there daily. After lunch, Devi used to take a little siesta, before going to the court in the afternoon. She listened to the complaints and problems of the subjects till the evening and used to solve their problems then and there.

Towards the evening, Devi would pass two hours in her prayer room worshipping God and studying. Then in the late evening she would once again attend the court and carry out administrative work. At that time, she used to listen to the letters and dictated reply to them. Thus only after finishing the day long chores, she would go to sleep.

Usually, her daily chores continued regularly like this. This routine would be changed slightly only when some special task arose like specific fast, festival or worship etc. Even then, she used to finish the administrative works of the day compulsively the same day. If she ever fell ill, she would carry out the administrative work from her bed.

She had a strong belief that God had given her that body and life only to discharge the duty fully, and not to waste. Hence, she spent every moment of her life in discharging her duty.

Even in her last days, and despite her failing health, Devi

Ahilya did hard work. It is apparent from the letter which the counsellor of Shrimant Peshwa had written to him barely six months prior to her death. He writes, "*Matushri* Ahilyabai had taken her evening bath and was chanting the rosary. When informed, she said that she would listen to the letters after dinner. That was the next day after the eclipse. Daylong fast and donations etc., had left her tired and exhausted. After the dinner, she held her court and then came to sit on her bed and summoned *Mantri* Rajeshri Vinayak Bajirao and Balaji Krishna to read out the letters that had arrived that day, to her."

"She stayed awake till a quarter past one and dictated the letters to the different *Kamavisdars* of the *Ghats* and the boats and got them dispatched. Those who resided nearby, were summoned themselves and issued orders. She herself made arrangement for the total footpaths of the *Ghats* of the Northern and Southern hills, checkposts, *chowkies*, fordes on both the banks of Narmada and upto the crossing point of Nemavur. She wrote letter to Rajeshri Raghunath Pant in Burharpur. She also wrote letters to *Kamavisdars*, landlords and landholders there and instructed them to make arrangements."

It is apparent from the letter, that even in her last days, when Devi had been completely exhausted physically and mentally, how she used to carry out the administrative work of the kingdom daily staying awake till one or two o'clock in late night.

25
Devi Ahilya: In the Eyes of the Savants

Devi Ahilya had become a legend right in her lifespan because of her dutifulness and moral conduct. Her religiosity, equitability, efficiency in administration, piety, contribution in constructions, gallantry, selflessness and motherly behaviour with the subjects had already won her a reputation and recognition among the masses as an ideal ruler throughout the country. Her subjects worshipped her as a pious *Lokmata*, while poets never tired in adoring her virtues.

Contemporary Sanskrit poet Khushali Ram writes about Devi—

Tasyaisa Kula Dakshni Kulapatemallari
—Ravasya Vai!
Dharmishtharthakari Snusha Shubhamat!
Stutya Tva Halyamidha ! !
Khanerav-Vadhu Sati Priyagnaa
Yatpara Luke Hitam!
Nityam Vaishnava Sadarvatam
Purvam Yatha Kurvati !!

(This dignified daughter-in-law of Malhar Rao, considerate, religious minded Ahilyabai was the wife of

Khande Rao. She was very meritorious and always engaged in the religious works for her summom bonum.)

Poet Khushali Ram writes further—

Nityam Sa Dadati Dananam Dev Brahmin
Puj Kana!
Kalam Vrat Yeti Sa Samyak Dharma Marg
Parayana!!

(She used to give donations to the Brahmins and the priests and pass her time in religious chores.)

Poet Khushali Ram also writes—

Kurukshetre Tirthe Tuladanameyam!
Suvarnat Maraupya Dikam Bara Baram!!
Ahilya Apisa Sandadav Danasheela!
Dhara Dev Tamya Guna Gya Nasheela!!

(Many times, she donated gold and silver equal to her weight in Kurukshetra. Virtuous and knowledgeable Ahilyabai had made great donations to the Brahmins.)

He has also written—

Deshe Deshe Cha Nityam Bamuvi Dhamamito
Danamannasya Samyak!
Pakva Pakvam Dadatyah Paramapi Bahudha
Danamarthan Nu Ru Pam!!
Daridrayam Yachakanam Bahuvi Dhamapi
—Yannir Gatam Tatprasan Gata!
Vachchha Purnrvabhu Vu Path Sharana
Gatanam Halya Bhidha Ya!!

(In all corners of the country, Devi Ahilya had donated many kinds of cereals. She fulfilled the pleas of the beggars and fulfilled the desires of anybody who came to her refuge.)

Kavi Moropant was a famous Marathi poet. No other poet

could match him in Maharashtra those days. In 1790, when Moropant visited the places of pilgrimage in Northern India, he was greatly moved to see the *Ghats*, hospices and cereal sheds built by Devi Ahilya in those places. On his return he specially visited Maheshwar to see Devi Ahilya.

During the pilgrimage, while taking bath in the Ganges, these lines spontaneously appeared on Moropant's lips—

Devi! Ahilyabai Yavi Bhetavayasa Satwar Ti!
To Punya Kirti He Hi Gange Doghi
Jani Hi Satwar Ti!!

(O Ganges! I will have a sight of Ahilyabai. Such as you are famous in the world, similarly she is, because both of you are beneficent for the world.)

Devi Ahilya was fully aware of the knowledge of Moropant. Hence, when he arrived in Maheshwar, Devi warmly welcomed and treated him very well. Moropant too was overwhelmed after seeing Devi. He stayed in Maheshwar for many days and closely observed the working style of Devi Ahilya. After he returned to Poona, he wrote a full volume of poems on Devi Ahilya, some of which are presented here—

Shri Harihar Bhakta Tum Devi Ahilye
Vara Dhara Bhusha!
Pusha Tuj Sadhu Mhene Khyata
Tuj Sama Na Vana Tanu Bhusha II-III
Devi Ahilyabai! Jhalis Jagatrayat
Tu Dhanya!
Na Nyay Dharma Nirata Anya Kalimaji
Alkili Kamya 1/2/1
Dharmath Gotra Janya Kinva
Jhalis Tu Dhara Janya!
Toj Devi Bhetali, Ji Satkirti

Kadhich He Na Rajanya 1/3/1
Jane Dharma Karina Tyas Stavito
Kuna Pundit Manya!
No Nyag-Dharma-Nirata Anya
Kalimaji Aikili Kanya 1/4/1
Na Tyajisi Narmadete Devi!
Tojhi Ti Bahu priya Ali!
Gange chi Hi Sakhi Ho ki Ubhaya
Manat Sat Kriya Ali 1/5/1
Shri Vishnupada! Stavili Tuad
Bhakta He Tula hi Manave!
Vishwa Jila Vanite Ka Na
Mayurenhi Tis Vanave 1/6/1

1. O Devi Ahilya! You are the supreme devotee of *Harihar*. With your devotion you have become a jewel on the earth. Even the Sun praises you. Daughter of Bana is not as famous as you are.

2. O Greatly honourable Devi! You are blessed in all the three worlds. No other woman is as equitable and pious as you are.

3. You are born to do religious service. You are possibly an incarnation of Parvati or Sita. No other king has such a reputation as you have.

4. Praised by the knowledgeable ones, which human being does not do religious services. But, O Devi! We have not heard about any other woman who is engaged in just and religious services in this *Kalyuga*.

5. You never part with Narmada because she is very dear to you. Both of you, are the dear friends of the Ganges because both of you like to engage in pious deeds.

6. O *Vishnupada*! Ahilyabai is a supreme devotee of yours. You will be pleased to know that every body adores

her. And when entire world praises her, why should Mayur (Moropant) not exalt her virtues.

One more star of Marathi literature, poet Prabhakar says in her adoration—

Sati Dhanya Dhanya Kalyugi Ahilyabai!
Gbeli Kirti Karuniya Bhumandala Che Thai!!
Maharaj Ahilyabai Punya Prani!
Sampurn Striyanmadhi Shreshtha Ratṇa khani!!
Darshane Mothya Papanchi Hoil Hani!
Jhadalt Roga Doshanchi Hoil Hani!!
Varniti Kirti Gatat Sant Te Gani!
Jhali Daivavashe Ti Holkarachi Rani!!

(Blessed is Ahilyabai, who is a *Sati* in *Kalyuga*. She has earned great reputation in the world. Pious Ahilyabai is an exquisite jewel among all the womenfolks. A mere glimpse of her is enough to destroy severe sins, serious diseases and faults. Saints sing in praise of this queen of Holkars.)

Famous English poetess of Scotish origin, Joana Bailey was a contemporary of Devi Ahilya. She had studied the works and ruling system of Devi in detail. She has, in fact, written a volume of poems on the personality of Devi Ahilya which contains beautiful description of Devi's virtues. Following lines depict that she was praised by all—

For thirty years her reign of peace
the land in blessings did increase
and she was blessed by every tongue
by stern and gentle... old and young.

She ruled for thirty years peacefully. In her regime, luxuries of the kingdom continued to increase. All kinds of people; polite, impolite, young and old, used to praise her open-heartedly.

Famous historian and political agent of East India Company in Central India, Sir John Malcom, had visited Central India a few years after the death of Devi Ahilya. In Maheshwar, he had met many companions of Devi Ahilya including Bharamal Dada and got some understanding of Devi's works. In his book *Memoir of Central India*, praising Devi, Sir Malcom writes—"Ahilyabai's nature was gentle and her rule extremely adorable. Her life shows clearly that having a devotion to the regulator of the universe and being dutiful cause practical benefits to a man."

In a letter to the king of Indore, Maharaj Hari Rao Holkar, after the first Afghan war, the then Viceroy of India Lord Eden Borough had described the greatness of Devi Ahilya and declared her as an excellent ideal and great ruler. Marathi litterateur Pt. Krishna Shastri Chiplunakar writes about Devi Ahilya—"All the mutually contrasting features are present in the nature of Ahilyabai. She was a woman, but she lacked the tendency of living in full make-up and adornment. Despite having unshakable faith in the religion of the self, she never hated the Muslims. Despite having been widowed in young age, she followed chastity with full faith. Despite being the mistress of inaccessible wealth, she lived her life like an expiator, and while she ruled her kingdom with full ability, she was completely free from ego. She feared only God. She had an extremely pure and gentle mind and never saw anybody with contempt. Instead she always worked to remove their faults. All this leads us to believe that in a human form, Devi Ahilyabai was an incarnation of a goddess."

Rai Bahadur Chintamani Vinayak Vaidya has been a famous historian of the South. In his article that had appeared in a Marathi magazine *Vividh Gyan Vistar* he writes about Devi Ahilya—"Because of her great virtues, this extraordinary woman was a jewel of not only Maharashtra, but of the entire

human race. She had comprehensive intelligence and hence was very careful and efficient in almost all the works. She was so generous in religion that in every field of religion and polity, her name is immortal. She was so magnanimous that no one in India comes anywhere near her in making donations. Her justice was so that thieves and money-lenders sought her blessings alike. She was so extraordinarily self-analysing and introspective that she did not allow anybody to praise her falsely. Her dominance was so hard that no one did anything without her permission, while she never dishonoured anybody. She had such a worshipping mind for Maratha empire that she always supported it. For the contemporary chieftains she had such a pure affection that she always wished well for them. She was so unavaricious that she never longed to usurp another kingdom, or recovered anything from her subjects and officials unlawfully in an unjust way. She was so kind that she did not ignore even the birds and animals from her pity. Her love for the subjects was so high that she regarded them as her own children."

Renowned historian Mr. Jadunath Sarkar regards Devi Ahilyabai as the greatest woman in history on the basis of the facts. He writes about Devi—"My respect for Devi Ahilyabai has increased. So far, I have been respecting her as an ascetic mother, who despite being a ruler and mistress of a great power and wealth, led a simple, spiritual life. She had got many temples and *Ghats* built and spent huge wealth in making donations and other religious activities, and gave away large lands and villages as reward. But now, a totally different aspect of her personality has been disclosed before me. From the original papers and letters, it becomes clear that she was a first-class politician, and that was why she readily extended her support to Mahadji. I have no hesitation in saying that without the support of Ahilyabai, Mahadji would never have gained so much importance in the politics of northern India."

Famous saint of modern age, Acharya Vinoba Bhave writes about Devi Ahilya—"Ahilya Devi was really indulged in religion. It had been a great experiment in the history of India when the administration of a kingdom was given into the hands of a religious minded woman. Those days, no one could have even thought that a widow could run a kingdom. But Marathas conducted such an experiment and gave the administration in the hands of Ahilyabai; and she ran the kingdom very-very successfully."

"Wherever we toured India, we heard about the good deeds of Ahilyabai. It has greatly influenced us. Many have attempted to conquer the world by arm power, but only a few have influenced the world with love and religion. Ahilya was one such person. She conquered all the provinces of India by her religiosity, intelligence and love. In the entire known history of India, I believe that Ahilyabai's place is second to none."

Nizam of Hyderabad, who was a contemporary of Ahilyabai, had written a condolence letter to Devi at the death of her grandson Nathyaba. He had addressed Devi as 'elder sister' in the letter. About Devi, Nizam had said, "Definitely no woman and no ruler is like Ahilyabai Holkar. Appropriating in a proper way, Ahilyabai had dedicated the wealth of late Malhar Rao and her country to God. In this, she is her own example."

Minister of Shrimant Madhav Rao Peshwa, and diplomat Nana Fadnavis, had said—"In sagacity and readiness to work, no one was ever close to her."

26

Devi Ahilya: Symbol of Woman Power

In Indian culture, woman has been regarded as a symbol of power. Our ancient religious scriptures, *Puranas* abound in examples of woman power. In ancient periods, when mighty warriors felt powerless before the enemies, they always invoked woman power, which invariably destroyed the monsters in the form of Durga or Kali. Lord Rama had also worshipped Shakti before waging a war against Ravana and was able to vanquish Ravana by her blessings.

Because of this form of woman power, women have enjoyed a supreme position of honour and respect. But during the middle ages, our culture became a victim of foreign cultural invasion, and the position of women continued to deteriorate slowly. Now the situation is so worse that the woman, who were once a symbol of power, came to be known as 'powerless', 'weak', 'frail', 'feeble' etc. In the name of securing and safeguarding her chastity many evil practices like veiling system, *Sati* and child marriage came into existence disguised as conventions in the male dominated society.

Although the position of common women might have weakened in the society because of prevailing circumstances, but the brilliance of womanhood has not completely vanished even today. Even in adverse conditions, Indian women have illumined the world again and again with their unearthly brilliance. Even in the modern age, the great woman power has assumed many names. Names like Lakshmibai, Jijabai, Meerabai, Durgawati, Kannaki, Chennama and Nivedita has not only influenced the society but also given it a new direction. It won't be exaggeration to describe Devi Ahilyabai as a complete incarnation of woman power and ability in the modern India. It was because of her extraordinary ability and dutifulness that despite an ordinary birth, Devi Ahilya came to be worshipped in her lifetime among the masses as *Lokmata, Sati* and *Devi.*

Devi Ahilyabai had a multifarious personality. She had all the pious virtues which are hard to be seen in a single person. A ruler may be religious, but he may lack in political and administrative abilities. If he is brave and powerful, then he may be cruel and merciless also. If he is wealthy, he might be lacking in good character and renunciation. If he is just, it is not necessary that he would be committed for the development of art and culture also. And if he is following the path of peace and goodwill, he might not be necessarily munificent. But in the life of Devi Ahilya, all these features are seen together. That is why she appears like a dynamic example of the power and ability of the Indian woman.

Among all the features of the Indian woman, features like internal strength, religiosity, motherly love, renunciation, love for art and culture are more or less present in every woman. All these features were present in Devi Ahilya, but at the same time she had features like administrative ability, gallantry, skill in warfare, diplomacy, justice, munificence etc., also. That is why she appears more excellent than any other contemporary ruler.

Struggles and pains of her life are rare in the life of an

ordinary person. One by one cruel blows of destiny hurt her. All the members of her family left her for their heavenly abode before her. Close companions and the so-called entrepreneurs of the society laid nothing but nails in her way. But Devi faced all these challenges with full capacity and brilliance because of her internal strength. She never bowed before the circumstances; never feared them nor gave away. She vanquished every crisis and challenge by her ability and strength. Instead of cursing the darkness that surrounded her, she lighted up her extraordinary life by her internal brilliance and not only dispelled the darkness of the society but illumined the life of her subjects with divine light of eternal pleasure.

In her time, women had a secondary position in the society. Path to progress was not available to them, while the male dominated society put many hurdles in their way. Despite all these hurdles, Devi defeated all the adversities by her strength and ability and established an ideal and benevolent kingdom. She is indeed a marvellous example of woman power and ability.

Great philosopher Plato had said— "Unless and until political sovereignty and philosophy come to be present in a single person, humanity can not be freed from its apparent evil saints."

Describing the virtues of an ideal king, Bheeshmacharya says in *Shanti Parva* of *Mahabharata*—

Atmabanshcha Jitkrodhah Shastrarth
Krit Ni Shchayah!
Dharme Charthe Cha Kamecha
Mokshecha Sa Ta Tam Ratah!!

(Only such a person deserves to be a king, who has curbed his mind, won the anger, understood the meaning of the scriptures correctly, and who is always ready to inculcate

Dharma, Artha, Kama and *Moksha*.)

Except the *Pauranic* kings like Dileep, Janak, Shri Rama, Shri Krishna or Yudhishthir, we don't see all these virtues present together in any king of the modern history. But a glance at the life of Devi Ahilya reveals beyond doubt that all these ideal virtues as described by Plato and Bheeshmacharya were present in her personality.

It is indeed a matter of great pleasure for the Indian women that, after thorough scrutiny of the long history of the world we find only one personality of *Lokmata* Devi Ahilya that represents an absolutely ideal ruler.

Name of Devi Ahilya has been written in golden words in the history of India because of her marvellous virtues and dutifulness. She can not be confined within the limits of any province, state or territory. She lives in the memory of entire Indian masses as a memorable, pious and venerable *Lokmata*. She is particularly a source of inspiration for the womenfolk of our country. Her life has become a valuable heritage for the entire humanity.

Appendix—1

Some Important Events in the Life of Devi Ahilya

Age	Event	Year
	Birth in the household of Manakoji Shinde of village Chauri, Taluka Ashti, district Beed, Maharashtra, on seventh day of darker phase of month Baisakh, Marathi calendar.	31-5-1725
8	Wedded to Khande Rao, son of Malhar Rao Holkar, the Subedar of Malwa.	1733
20	Gave birth to son Maley Rao.	1745
23	Gave birth to daughter Muktabai.	1748
29	Death of husband in the battle of Khumbher. Ahilyabai got ready to become *Sati*, but forced to change her decision because of pitiable pleas by her father-in-law.	24-3-1754
36	Death of mother-in-law Gautamabai.	29-9-1761

41	Death of father-in-law Malhar Rao Holkar in Alampur. Got the rights of Subedari for the son Maley Rao.	25-5-1766
42	Death of son Maley Rao. Taking over the reigns of the kingdom and getting the rights of Subedari of Malwa transferred to a relative and commander-in-chief Tukoji Rao. Invasion by Raghoba Peshwa on Indore; compelled to return without a war just by the sheer intelligence and fearlessness. Daughter Muktabai gave birth to a son Nathyaba.	1767
55	Marriage of grandson Nathyaba.	1780
59	Death of brother Shahaji Shinde.	1784
61	Death of brother Mahadji Shinde.	1786
65	Untimely death of grandson Nathyaba and becoming *Sati* of his wives.	15-11-1790
66	Sudden death of the son-in-law Yashwant Rao Fanase due to cholera and committing of *Sati* by his wives including Muktabai.	3-11-1791
70	Journey of Devi Ahilya's life comes to an end in Maheshwar on *Shavan Badi* *Saka* era 1717.	13-8-1795

Appendix—2

Incomplete List of the Construction Work Done by Devi Ahilya

Ambagaon	:	Arranged for the lightings in the temples.
Ayodhya	:	Built a Shri Rama temple.
Amarkantak	:	Built a hospice.
Anand Kanan	:	Got the restoration of Vishweshwar (Jyotirling) temple done.
Alampur	:	Established a public kitchen. Built a temple of Harihareshwar at the spot where father-in-law Malhar Rao died. Built a canopy commemorating father-in-law and a temple of Khande Rao Martand opposite to canopy.
Ujjain	:	Built a temple of Chintamani Ganapati and arranged for the worship in Mahakaleshwar temple.
Rishikesh	:	Built many temples.
Onkar (Mandhata)	:	Built a temple of Amaleshwar, a garden and a canopy. Got the construction of Gauri Somnath temple completed,

		which had been started by her mother-in-law Gautamabai.
Karnataka	:	Arranged for the help of the poor.
Kashi	:	Built the famous Manikarnika *Ghat* in October 1785 at a cost of Rs. 25000. Built Dashashwamegh *Ghat* in the same year. Built a new *Ghat* also. Got Kashi Vishweshwar temple restored. Built two huge temples Gautameshwar and Ahilyodwarkeshwar.
Kurukshetra	:	Built the *Ghat* and temple.
Kedarnath	:	Built a hospice and a sump on top of a mountain for the benefit of the pilgrims.
Kolhapur	:	Arranged for the worship in temple.
Gangottari	:	Built four temples—Vishwanath, Kedarnath, Bhairava and Annapurna, and six hospices. Got many hospices built on the hilly-routes.
Gaya	:	Got a Vishnu temple restored. This temple houses a beautiful idol of black stone.
Chinchwad	:	Arranged for the alms for the poors.
Chikhalata	:	Set up a cereal shed for the pilgrims circumambulating Narmada.
Chitrakoot	:	Set up a Rama Panchayatan.
Chauri	:	Built a temple of Mahadev and a *Ghat*. Temple's name is Ahilyeshwar. Eight hundred rupees are sent annually from Indore.
Chhondi	:	Built a temple.
Jagannathpuri	:	Donated some villages to the priest of the temple to worship in the main temple.

Jaongaon	:	Helped monastery of Ramdas Swami.
Jamghat	:	Built a beautiful gateway.
Jejuri	:	Built a temple of Martand.
Tonki	:	Arranged for the donation of money.
Tarana	:	Built an ancient Shiv temple named Tilbhandereshwar.
Trayambak	:	This place is situated 10 km away from Nasik in Maharashtra. It has been built with stones and has enchanting pond and two temples.
Devaprayag	:	Situated in Himalayas *en route* to Gangottari. A river Alaknanda converges here with the Ganges. This village (Devaprayag) is situated at an altitude of 2236 ft. A public kitchen of Ahilyabai is still operational.
Dwarka	:	Known as Dwaravati or Dwarika also. Some villages donated to the priest to carry out worship etc.
Daru Kanan	:	Arranged for the worship in Nageshwar temple.
Nathdwara	:	Built a hospice.
Nasik	:	Built a Shri Rama temple.
Niphal	:	Also called Niphar. Built a sump *en route* to Dindori village.
Nilkanth Mahadev	:	Built a *Shivalay*, which is famous as Neel-Kanth Mahadev. A beautiful Gomukh built by Devi is also here.
Naimisharanya	:	Built a *Marhi* of Mahadev, a hospice, a *Ghat* and sump here.
Parali	:	Got the temple of Baijnath restored.
Pantharpur	:	Built Shri Rama temple and helped many people by donations.

Prayag	:	Built a huge *Ghat*.
Pushkar	:	Built a temple and a hospice.
Paitham	:	Built a cereal shed.
Punatambe	:	Built a *Ghat*.
Badrinarayan	:	Built a temple of Hari, a hospice and many sumps. A public kitchen of Devi is also running here.
Bithur	:	Built Brahma *Ghat*.
Beed	:	This village is in Aurangabad, Maharashtra. Got an old *Ghat* restored.
Bhusawal	:	Built a temple.
Mandaleshwar	:	Town stands on the bank of Narmada in Khargaon district of M.P. Devi built a *Ghat* and a Shiv temple here.
Mathura	:	Built a hospice.
Maheshwar	:	Has been the capital of Ahilyabai. She built many *Ghat*, temples, and canopies here. Established a public kitchen where food is given to the poor. During the time of Ahilyabai, religious ceremonies used to be held every year in the month of *Savan*.
Rameshwar	:	Built a hospice and set up a cereal shed.
Raver	:	Built a temple.
Vrindavan	:	Set up a cereal shed, and built a stepwell of red stones, which has fifty-seven flights of steps.
Verul	:	Got the restoration of a temple Ghrishneshwar, which was built by Gautamabai. Built a sump.
Shrishail	:	Built a Shiv temple of Mallikarjuna.
Sangamner	:	Built a Rama temple.
Satara	:	Got a well dug in Mahadev temple.

Saptashringgarh	:	Built a hospice.
Sultanpur (Khandesh)	:	Built temples.
Sulpeshwar	:	Set up a cereal shed and built a huge temple of Mahadev. Every visitor is given a blanket and round water-pot here.
Somnath	:	Also known by other names like Devapattan, Prabhaspattom, Pattom Somanath, Somanath Pattom. Mentioned as Prabhas in *Mahabharata*. Mahadev temple of Somnath is famous in history. Mahmud of Ghazni had demolished it in 1024. Devi got it restored and the idol resurrected.
Haridwar	:	In the north western direction, and towards the South of Kushavart Har Ki Pauri, there is huge *Ghat* on the bank of the Ganges. Devi built a hospice on the same *Ghat*.
Handiya	:	Situated on the bank of Narmada in Madhya Pradesh. Devi built a hospice and temple of Sidhnath here. This 60–70 feet high temple is built of brown stones. Devi built a huge *Ghat* also, and set up a cereal shed.

Apart from these major works, Devi set up many cereal sheds in small and big villages and built hospices for the pilgrims throughout the country. In her time, she got the restoration of uncountable temples done. She also arranged to distribute food and water to the needy.

Appendix—3

Devi Ahilyabai made arrangements for the distribution of the holy water of the Ganges every year at following places—

(1) Rameshwar, (2) Mallikarjuna, (3) Janardana Vasudev (Mysore), (4) Padmanath Janardan, (5) Abhishayan Anant Shayan, (6) Balaji Giri, (7) Gokaran Mahabateshwar, (8) Subrahmaneshwar, (9) Pashupateshwar (Nepal), (10) Dwarikanath, (11) Dakornath, (12) Utkanteshwar, Mahadev, (13) Avandya Jagannath, (14) Parali Vaijnath, (15) Tyambakeshwar, (16) Rama Panchawati, (17) Matrigaya Siddheshwar, (18) Bheem Shankar, (19) Pantharpur, (20) Ekaling Mahadev, (21) Kapil Muni, (22) Kedareshwar, (23) Sorathi Somanath, (24) Nathdwara, (25) Vishweshwar Mahadev, (26) Girgeshwar, (27) Loteshwar (28) Jejuri, (29) Ujjain, (30) Maheshwar, (31) Omkareshwar, (32) Benaras, (33) Badri Kedareshwar, (34) Jadakhandi.

Appendix—4

Poet Khushali Ram has presented a list of the places of pilgrimage in his book of verses where Devi Ahilya had carried out construction works.

Ayodhya, Mathura, Maya, Kanchi, Kashinath, Brahanan!
Pushkarsthan, Kurukshetra, Dwarikashrit Bhusuran!!
Gaya, Prayag Ramadri, Sukshetrottam Sanshritan!
Jambu-Margathitanchapi, Tamraparm Samashritan!!
Avantika, Sthitanvipranpujayamas Sarvada!
Tathaiva Devatansadhvi Pujayamas Bhaktitah!!
Skand Shrivyankateshanch Shri Rangesh Maha Prabhum!
Ananta Shayinam, Devam, Setu Rameshwaram Haram!!
Kamanatham Tathan Kareshwaramdivyam Maha Prabhum!
Maha Kalishwaram Devam, Kashi Vishweshwaram Prabhum!!
Jagannath Swayam Divyam Tathach Badrishwaram!
Shrimant Keshavam Devam Jambumargeshwaram Shivam!!
Pandurangam Vitthalakhyam Gokarneshshivam Tatha!
Govardhanadharam Natham Ekalingabhidham Shivam!!
Durga Lambodaram Bhanum Shivam Narayan Prabhum!
Pujayamas Dharmagya Sarvatra Pratimamyam !!

Yeshu-Yeshucha Desheshu Yadyatirth Smashritan!
Shri Mallari Ravasya Smusha Dharmvati Chasa!!
Tirthe-Tirthecha Sarvatra Devandevanhi Bhurishah!
Preshayamas Satpritya Varshikam Chapyupuyanam!!

Appendix—5

Description of major *Ghats* built by Devi Ahilya throughout the country

Sl. No.	Place	Name of the Ghat	Dimension (in feet)
1.	Varanasi	1. Dashashmegh or Ahilya Ghat	190.6 × 70.0
		2. Manikarnika Ghat	147.0 × 66.0
		3. Special Ghat for women	68.0 × 95.0
2.	Ayodhya, Ghat on Saryu	Ghat No. 1	110.2 × 42.10
		Ghat No. 2	50.0 × 112.0
3.	Haridwar near Har ki Pauri	Kushwant Ghat	128.5 × 65.4
4.	Mathura	Kaliyadeh Ghat	100.0 × 80.0
5.	Prayag		175.00 × 100
6.	Mandaleshwar		228.0 × 120
7.	Handiya	Ghat on Narmada	200.0 × 150
8.	Punatamba Dist. Auranga-bad, Maharashtra	Ghat on Godawari	120.0 × 75.0
9.	Chauri (Place of birth of		

	Ahilyabai)	Ghat on Sina river	200 ft.
10.	Nasik	Ghat built opposite Vishweshwar temple	150 ft.
11.	Important *Ghats* of Maheshwar	1. Ahilya Ghat	150.0 × 291.0
		2. Raja Rajeshwar Ghat	171.0 × 76.0
		3. Kashi Vishweshwar	105.0 × 100.0
		4. Peshwa Ghat	121.0 × 150.0
		5. Bharmal Dada Ghat	45.0 × 18.0
		6. Sardar Fanase Ghat	96.0 × 47.0

Note: Apart from the above mentioned *Ghats* in Maheshwar, reference of 22 more *Ghats* is also available, all of which in the names of Tiharum, Gangaram Zamindars. Moreover, there are *Ghats* built by other Holkar kings also. Reference of Lakshmikund and Panchkund built by Ahilyabai in Kurukshetra and Brahmin *Ghat* of Bithur is also available.

□□□